THE COTTON DUST PAPERS

Science, Politics, and Power in the "Discovery" of Byssinosis in the U.S.

by
Charles Levenstein
and
Gregory F. DeLaurier

with Mary Lee Dunn

I0075134

Work, Health, and Environment Series
Series Editors: Charles Levenstein and John Wooding

Baywood Publishing Company, Inc.
AMITYVILLE, NEW YORK

Library of Congress Catalog Number: 2001043095
ISBN: 0-89503-265-1 (cloth)

Library of Congress Cataloging-in-Publication Data

The cotton dust papers : science, politics, and power in the "discovery" of byssinosis in the U.S. / by Charles Levenstein and Gregory F. DeLaurier, with Mary Lee Dunn.
    p. cm. - - (Work, health and environment series)
    Includes bibliographical references and index.
    ISBN 0-89503-265-1 (cloth)
    1. Byssinosis- -United States- -History. 2. Textile workers- -Diseases- -United States- -History. I. Levenstein, Charles. II. DeLaurier, Gregory F., 1949- III. Dunn Mary Lee. IV. Series

RC775.B9 C685 2001
616.2'44- -dc21   2001043095

Cover photograph: Portrait of Louis Harrell, a cotton textile worker for 44 years, three weeks before his death from byssinosis in 1978. Courtesy of Earl Dotter. earldotter@erols.com

Dedication

We dedicate this book to the late Dr. Arend Bouhuys whose commitment to workers' health and unflagging determination to uncover the secret of byssinosis make of his life a model and inspiration for all workplace health and safety professionals, and indeed for anyone who believes the struggle for justice is a worthy endeavor. This book is also a tribute to those American textile workers who for scores of years suffered a malady that came out of their work but whose illness went unrecognized, unhelped, and uncompensated. May this book contribute to it never happening again. We remember them.

Foreword

This study was launched with the support and interest of David Wegman and Barbara Rosenkrantz when I was on leave from the University of Connecticut and enjoying a NIOSH traineeship at Harvard School of Public Health. Everett Mendelson in Harvard's History of Science Department further encouraged the work. Ian Greaves, now at the University of Minnesota, Les Boden, now at Boston University School of Public Health, and Margaret Quinn, now at UMass Lowell, were important participants in the intellectual ferment that contributed to the study. Our ad hoc "seminar on the history of occupational lung diseases," sponsored by the Occupational Health Program and the History of Science Department, involved graduate students and some faculty in what was ostensibly an antiquarian discussion, but one which rapidly became political. Financial support from NIOSH enabled me to continue to work on the project at Harvard and to continue to commute to the University of Connecticut in Hartford. At UConn, the interest of Peter Barth, Russ Farnen, and Ray Elling permitted me to give time and energy to this study. Over the years, the critical reading by Eve Spangler of Boston College, John Wooding of UMass Lowell, Dom Tuminaro of NYCOSH, and other friends, colleagues, and students have been important to me and to this work. I know no way to estimate the value of the moral and intellectual support of Fred Sperounis of UMass Lowell for me and for this project.

One great contribution to the work occurred on the day that Mark Ayanian, a student at University of North Carolina, provided me with the documents concerning Peter Shrag's experience in North Carolina. Another boost to the work came from Ira Burnim and the Southern Poverty Law Center when they asked me to serve as an expert witness in a brown lung case in Alabama. The hospitality and interest of Len Stanley, Chip Hughes, and Charlotte Brody, as well as the Brown Lung Association in Alabama, were important to me. I owe a great debt to the textile workers of Opelika, which I hope this book will help to pay.

The libraries and librarians at Yale University and Harvard University, particularly Countway Library and Baker Library, provided advice and great service.

Last, but not least, I would like to acknowledge that a kernel of inspiration for this work came from the 1950s research of Skipper Hammond on textile worker organizing in the South.

Charles Levenstein

v

Preface

WORK, HEALTH AND ENVIRONMENT SERIES
Series Editors: **Charles Levenstein and John Wooding**

While we stand at the beginning of a new millennium, it is clear that the brave talk of a new era is—for many—the empty rhetoric of promises unfulfilled. Around the world workers and communities are increasingly the victims of unsafe workplaces and polluted environments. In all countries, too many remain without jobs or under-employed. In the United States, many workers need more than one job to lift themselves beyond the poverty level. In much of Europe, unemployment rates appear to be intractably high. In Asia and much of the developing world, workers are slaving in factories at wages that are appallingly low. In Africa, ravaged by AIDS and war, only the lucky few can still put bread on the table. In most of the globe, the threat of environmental catastrophe, the erosions of indigenous cultures, and exploitation of workers continues unabated. Recurrent economic crises continue to threaten those who have made small gains and stability can only be achieved with loans from the IMF and international capital that come with stringent conditions. In the era of the triumph of the market, all is not well.

This is not to say that gains have not been made. Medical advances and public health initiatives have ended the fear of disease and early death for many. Standards of living have improved for some, and the awareness of threats to health and environment has made many more willing to fight for healthy lives. But much remains to be done and the "free marketeers" attack the role that democracy and government can play in protecting the lives of citizens throughout the world. The "market" cannot solve all these problems. The "market" never will.

So, does this mean that there is nothing we can do? Of course not. Rather, that we have an especially difficult task ahead. We must understand this era with good analysis and innovative strategies. We cannot look back to a golden progressive age or halcyon socialist past, nor can we forget the lessons we learned. What we must do is engage and understand what is going on in the world, and develop and propose viable alternatives and progressive strategies. This in essence is the purpose of this book series and the point of our focus.

We have titled the series *Work, Health, and Environment.* The conjunction of topics is deliberate and critical. We begin at the point of production. Work is essential to all our lives. Work is where things are made, good things as well as bad things. While work brings income and meaning, it also brings danger and threats to health. The point of production is where goods and services are produced but it is also the source of environmental contamination and pollution. In other words, work, health, and environment are intimately linked. In this series we will publish works that analyze and describe the relationship between what goes on in the workplace, the consequences for the public health, and environmental degradation. We define health and environment broadly. Health is not limited to the absence of disease or to individual health. It must also mean a healthy and sustainable economy, a democratic and participatory politics, a workplace where the rights of workers are respected and enforced, and communities that are sustainable, crime free, and nurturing of the physical and mental health of all.

Acknowledgments

I would like to thank first and foremost Charles Levenstein who invited me to join this project and help bring it to fruition. Also, it is primarily his research, along with that of William Mass and Susan Woskie, that is the foundation of this work. I would like to thank Mary Lee Dunn whose earlier draft of this book made the final writing a far easier task than it might have been. Both Charles and Mary Lee have been a pleasure to work with. I would also like to thank the faculty of the Work Environment Department at UMass Lowell who welcomed me into their midst and taught me much. Thanks also to the Boston Editorial Collective of the journal *Capitalism, Nature, and Socialism* for reading early chapters of this work and offering helpful criticism as well as encouragement, and to two anonymous reviewers for Baywood for their insightful comments. John Wooding has been a friend, colleague, and political ally for well over two decades. His wise counsel and generous encouragement have made an immeasurable contribution to my work here and at so many other times in my life. Finally, my deepest gratitude to my wife, Jeannette Frey, whose patience and support gave me the time and confidence to complete this project.

Gregory F. DeLaurier

It has been and is a pleasure to work with Charles Levenstein and Greg DeLaurier on this and other projects. For a dozen years now I have worked with Chuck Levenstein on the journal *New Solutions* and on various book manuscripts and other projects. For me, it has been not only a fruitful collaboration, but also a journey of discovery and an education in the world of the workplace, policy-making, and the political economy of work. It has been a rewarding time. Greg DeLaurier took up this unfinished manuscript and made it more than it was with his graceful writing and sensitivity to what it needed.

To my other colleagues in the Department of Work Environment at the University of Massachusetts Lowell goes my gratitude for sharing their world of work and science.

Thank you to my sons, Daniel and Justin Maguire, who tolerate and support my many projects and interests even when it sometimes means that mine get priority over their own. Their turn comes.

Mary Lee Dunn

Table of Contents

But face it, the money is the most important thing. It's a living. It represents your home and your food and your clothes and everything. And when you're not trained for nothing else . . . even if you were trained the situation's not available. And more or less you just have to go on.

—*Mrs. Clara Lewis,* former textile worker

If they are working in the mills, they must know it's dangerous.

—*Melvin B. Bradshaw,* former president Liberty Mutual Insurance

A worker in the cotton bale opening room of a textile mill, Ware Shoals, South Carolina, 1978. Earl Dotter

CHAPTER 1

By Any Other Name: Brown Lung and the Social Recognition of Disease

AN AMERICAN TRAGEDY

Byssinosis is an occupational disease. A simple sentence, really, a straightforward statement of fact. Yet, hidden within this statement lies a fifty-year history of struggle to have industry and science in the United States utter these words, acknowledge their truth. We ask in this book what this struggle was about and why it was so protracted. What took so long?

Byssinosis—or "brown lung," the now colloquial term for the disease coined by social reformer Ralph Nader in the 1970s—is a disease of cotton mill workers. It is caused by the inhalation of cotton dust. The symptoms are chest tightness, shortness of breath, coughing and wheezing. At the earliest stage of the disease, these symptoms appear on the first workday after an absence from work. At a later stage, a worker will exhibit these symptoms on second and subsequent workdays. Eventually, the disease progresses to the point where a worker experiences chronic shortness of breath and other severe respiratory problems. These symptoms do not abate even when the worker is no longer exposed to cotton dust; in retirement, the condition of the worker only continues to worsen.

Brown lung is not a fatal disease in the same sense that cancer frequently is. A worker-victim may live for some years until his heart, deprived of oxygen, gives out; or until she catches pneumonia and her weakened condition can offer little resistance. There remains no cure for brown lung once the disease has moved beyond the early reversible stage.

Prior to the 1970s, years of laboring in cotton textile plants had left tens of thousands of workers crippled and poor; generations of mill workers had suffered the agony of this disease alone and ignored. In 1977, Dr. Arend Bouhuys, at the time the leading expert in the United States on byssinosis, estimated that 35,000

1

mill workers, both active and retired, were suffering from severe lung impairment due to brown lung [1]. The Occupational Safety and Health Administration (OSHA) has accepted this figure and added that as many as 100,000 workers were then at risk from cotton dust exposure [2].

The sad and infuriating point to these casualty figures is that they might have been avoided. Simple control of the level of cotton dust to which the worker could be exposed could have spared these workers the prolonged suffering that is byssinosis. But such control did not come into existence until it was too late.

Even though textiles is the oldest industry in the United States, having been around since the early decades of the nineteenth century when Henry Cabot Lowell stole the textile manufacturing technology from England and set up shop on the shores of the Merrimack River in Massachusetts; even though as early as 1837 the harmful effects of cotton dust were known and noted in the United States; even though in Great Britain byssinosis had been recognized and fully described by 1936 and a compensation scheme for sick textile workers had been enacted in 1940; even though in at least three instances in the United States from the 1930s to the 1960s strong evidence suggested the existence of brown lung in cotton textile mills, not until 1969 did the medical community in the United States acknowledge that byssinosis was indeed a disease.

The subsequent campaign to control cotton dust became part of the successful effort to adopt a new Federal Occupational Safety and Health Act in 1970 which led to the creation of OSHA in 1971. Still, OSHA did not issue a standard covering worker exposure to cotton dust until 1976, a standard the textile industry challenged all the way up to the Supreme Court, and the textile industry, on the whole, did not admit publicly that there was a problem in their mills until the late 1970s.

Why did this all happen, or perhaps more accurately, why did so much not happen? How could it be that in an advanced industrial democracy with a medicine wedded to the latest in technology and a scientific community second to none, a relatively obvious and easy-to-prevent occupational disease could go for so long unacknowledged and its victims unprotected and uncompensated? What took so long?

BYSSINOSIS AND PRODUCTION

Brown lung is the result of the economic-technological process of producing cotton textiles. You don't get byssinosis in a polyester factory. You probably don't get it unless you work in certain parts of the textile mill which are particularly dusty, and you probably won't get it even in these places if the plant is adequately ventilated, which few were in the United States prior to the late 1970s and 1980s.

Cotton dust contains within it an array of substances, including ground up plant matter, non-cotton matter, pesticides, soil, fungi, bacteria. The specific component or components of cotton dust that cause byssinosis have yet to be isolated, although the likely culprit is "bract," a toxic substance present within the cotton plant. In any event, there no longer is any dispute over the link between breathing in cotton dust and contracting brown lung.

OSHA now has in place strict PELs, permissible exposure limits, covering the amount of cotton dust that may be in the air in the workplace. OSHA also requires that employers take regular dust measurements, install dust controls, and provide respirators when such controls are not sufficient to reduce exposure. Employees who work in dusty areas must have free annual medical exams, including breathing tests, and training programs concerning the dangers of cotton dust must be conducted annually [3]. But it must be remembered that all of these requirements and safeguards are of recent origin, while the dangers of cotton dust existed and were known about far earlier.

The making of cotton textiles begins out in the field with the harvesting of the cotton. This is not a dusty operation and it's outside work, so field workers are not at risk of getting brown lung. Cotton picking technology, however, may well have an impact on mill workers. Mechanical picking generally means dirtier cotton, cotton contaminated with foreign material, and the bract that is the possible cause of brown lung.

Cotton ginning, the next step in preparing the natural fibers for textile production, cleans out some of the contaminants, although the central purpose of ginning is to remove cotton seed from the fiber. Ginning is a dusty process, but it's a seasonal operation and workers are not subject to the daily, year-in and year-out assault on the lungs that cotton mill workers can experience. Repeated ginning will take out more of the problematic contaminants, but will also weaken the fiber, so economics limits the amount of cleaning that will happen at the gin. After ginning, cotton lint is compressed, baled, and shipped off to the textile mills.

At the mill, further preparation of cotton includes the manufacture of thread from the fiber and the manufacture of cloth from the thread. In order to make the thread, the covers of the bales have to be removed, the bales opened, and materials loosened. At this stage, different kinds of cotton are mixed together and further cleaning and loosening occurs.

This is incredibly dusty work and in most modern plants is totally automated; so under ideal conditions few workers are exposed to serious hazards. Historically, however, the earliest in-plant processes—opening, beating or "scrutching," and the next operation, "carding"—have posed the most serious threats to the health of textile workers.

Carding is a continuation of the process that leads to thread. The cotton is cleaned further, short fibers are removed, and a long "sliver" is created which will go on for further combing. Carding is itself a dusty process, but the cleaning of the card machine parts, "stripping" and "grinding," are even worse, giving rise to early names for byssinosis among workers, such as "grinders asthma."

Combing of the slivers gets out more of the dirt and other contaminants, straightens out the long fibers, and continues to get rid of the shorter ones. At the end of this process, the sliver is ready to be converted into thread via spinning. Spinning is not considered to be a terribly dusty process, but sufficient exposures remain to make ventilation an important issue; spinners do get byssinosis.

A variety of other thread-finishing activities make the product ready for weaving into cloth, but they do not appear to be relevant to textile worker lung disease. It is the early cotton mill processes that are extremely dusty and that pose such serious problems for worker health.

THEORETICAL CONCERNS

Occupational disease and injury occur within and because of a particular social, political, and economic setting [4] (for further elaboration see [5, 6]). In broadest terms, we wish here to examine this setting and its effect on the course of the discovery of byssinosis in the United States, but offer first the theoretical perspectives that will guide our investigations.

We begin with the simple and incontestable fact that working conditions strongly affect the health of those who work within those conditions; if a worker suffers an industrial disease or injury it is because of the work he or she is doing. Occupational disease and injury thus remain distinct from other health problems in that they are the direct result of economic activity. The worker produces disease and injury just as surely as he or she produces the end product of production. To say otherwise is a semantic sleight of hand, akin to separating the beneficial effects of a medicine from its side effects: in both cases, a single entity is creating an array of inseparable outcomes.

Within capitalist relations of production, owners and managers privately control productive assets. This means, among many other things, that the technical organization of production—what is produced, how it is produced, when it is produced, at what rate, with what raw materials, with what tools, the physical configuration of the workplace—will be decided by these groups. Lacking ownership rights, workers will have no say in these decisions.

As capitalism is a competitive system, owners and managers must maximize profit and so technical decisions will be made on the basis of efficiency. This in turn means that capitalists must be able to both minimize costs and effectively control the labor process. Both goals are inimical to making workplace health and safety a primary concern.

Workplace health and safety is, first of all, expensive and threatens competitiveness by threatening to reduce profits. Owners and managers may not purposely set out to ruin the health of workers, but as Levenstein and Wooding point out, "it may be *absolutely* necessary to do so in order to make money [or] *relatively* necessary to do so because other more expensive ways of producing result in *less* money" [7, p. 3].

Owners and managers must control the labor process as it is the only way they can insure that this process remains constructed toward the sole end of maximizing profits. Workplace health and safety thus not only directly threatens profits, but also *indirectly* does so when health and safety demands are made by labor or the state. The struggle over workplace health and safety becomes a class struggle, and owners and managers will resist—and have resisted—such imprecations with all the power at their disposal.

All of this puts owners and managers in direct confrontation with occupational health professionals—occupational physicians and nurses, scientists, epidemiologists, and industrial hygienists. Their purpose, after all, is to identify workplace health and safety problems, their causes and cures. Such activity, however, can have enormous financial consequences. If, for instance, the respiratory problems of cotton mill workers are blamed on "chronic bronchitis" due to smoking, there is no industry culpability or obligation; if however the same malady is found to derive from "byssinosis" caused by breathing in cotton dust, industry will face the cost of compensation and prevention as well as open itself up to possible outside intervention into control of the workplace. Much is at stake, then, in the relation between occupational health practitioners and capital, and it is this particular relation we focus on in this work.

Occupational health investigators, like all of us, live in society, are its creatures, and their work is a social task, albeit sometimes undertaken in solitude. But to say this is not to deny the importance of scientific work—we do not offer here a postmodern screed against the scientific method—nor the possibility of scientific integrity. Nonetheless, the ethics of health science are worked out in the context of power, economics, culture, and the social codes and assumptions this context entails. "Scientific objectivity," in this view, is an impossibility, as science must negotiate with and within this context; consciously or not, confront it or comply with it.

In the history of the United States there quite clearly exists the predominance of a *laissez-faire*, liberal ideology sympathetic toward and celebratory of the unfettered growth of private capital and industrial development, and antithetical to government intervention. Occupational health and safety has evolved and operates within this hegemonic ideology, and has resulted in what Daniel Berman has called the "compensation-safety apparatus" among industry, insurers, professional organizations, standard setting institutes, and other organizations and groups involved in worker health and safety [8]. Within the context of a claimed neutrality between labor and managers, this compensation-safety apparatus stresses private sector control over government regulation of the workplace, cooperative rather than confrontational and private rather than public approaches to workplace problems, and an overarching concern for minimizing cost.

With this apparatus in place, the dilemma faced by occupational health investigators is quite clear: if the ethics of public health call for the open investigation and public disclosure of an industrial health problem and an unwavering commitment to the well-being of those affected by this problem, these are precisely the kinds of things the compensation-safety apparatus is meant to forestall. So a delicate negotiation must be performed by investigators as they pursue their work, for the costs are high.

A key element of control that owners and managers have in their relations with occupational health care investigators is their power over access to the workplace. Scientists cannot study disease if they cannot access, identify, and examine the diseased and look at their environment. As the "gatekeepers" of the workplace, employers can exact concessions from investigators that may limit the scope and impact of their work. Access for investigators may mean giving up control of their work, allowing employers to review their work and maintain veto power over the publication of their findings. If an investigator chooses to violate such conditions, she may not only face the wrath of employers but also that of her own superiors and supervisors convinced of the necessity of a professional ethos of quiet cooperation with industry. The investigator then must be mindful of career advancement, professional reputation, and the desire for material security. Finally, he must keep in mind the need for funding, and how his actions will affect future funding, particularly from industry but also from other sources.

Thus must occupational health professionals balance their research concerns and ethical considerations against and within a hegemonic apparatus and the power of employers, and the complex web of economic, political, and social relations these engender. It is no easy task.

The task might be made easier if a counter-hegemonic social force exists, in a context where the power of employers is effectively challenged. Such a context would both serve as a support for health investigators against employers and also challenge the workplace autonomy of employers.

Obviously, such a counter-hegemonic force is organized labor, but, in general, unions in the United States have never been strong, by necessity often operating from a defensive and protective posture, and have never been able to significantly and consistently challenge the workplace prerogatives of owners and managers. This is not to say that organized labor has had no effect in improving the workplace, it has, but this effect has been episodic rather than sustained, incremental rather than transformative.

At this point it is fair to ask, if occupational health investigators are, in a sense, cowed and labor weak, how is it that any improvement in workplace health and safety occurs? Our thesis is that there are particular historical periods in which progressive social forces coalesce to form a strong alliance in support of workplace reforms, and it is during these periods that the most significant progress in such reforms occurs. When labor is able to combine forces with occupational and public health professionals as well as with other citizen or grassroots organizations, such as those concerned with the environment, when such a coalition receives popular recognition and support, a generally favorable press, and a reasonably attentive government, then real pressure can be brought to bear on owners and managers. Yet, as we explain below, given the realities of ownership relations in this country, the effect of such pressure may be indirect.

Why would employers act to protect the health and safety of workers? Altruistic concern for the well-being of a fellow human is not beyond the realm of possibility here, but such Fezziwig-like inclinations do not and cannot escape the fact that under capitalism "profit is both the necessary and limiting condition for the pursuit of all other goals" [9, see also 10]. Self-interest and economic rationality, then, are more likely causes of employer concern for health and safety. Self-interest and economic rationality, however, are not predefined terms and may very much depend on the social forces within which they operate and evolve.

Employers may act on health and safety issues to blunt union influence, forestall unionization, or prevent government regulation. They may also act to diffuse public outcry over media attention to health hazards, to create a public image of socially responsible "corporate citizens" and protect profits. Such response, though, obviously depends on there being public attention and media outcry in the first place and hence the activism that produces them.

Finally, and perhaps most importantly, in a situation where owners and managers face intense pressure for change, competition itself may determine a firm's attitude toward health and safety. More technologically advanced firms can upgrade for health and safety at a relatively lower cost than smaller, more technologically primitive competitors. When they do so—effectively breaking ranks with other firms in the industry—leading firms not only reap a public relations reward but may impose on lesser competitors costs they can ill afford, especially if such upgrades become mandatory through government regulations, regulations that leading firms may actually collude with government in creating. It is also in this context that leading firms are most likely to allow occupational health investigators access to the workplace and where the science developed by studies and research will have the greatest impact. In a situation where private control of the workplace is strong and labor weak, such breaking of ranks spurred on by activist pressure may be key to workplace reform.

THE STORY OF BROWN LUNG:
AN OVERVIEW

The problem of cotton dust in the mills is not a new one. A Pittsburgh physician, testifying before the Pennsylvania Senate in 1837, reported on conditions in cotton mills:

> The factories are ill ventilated; their atmosphere is constantly impregnated and highly surcharged with the most offensive effluvia—arising from the persons of the inmates, and the rancid oils applied to the machinery . . . In the rooms where the cotton wool undergoes the first process of carding and breaking, the atmosphere is one floating mass of cotton particles, which none

but those accustomed to it, can breathe, for an hour together, without being nearly suffocated [11, pp. 181-182].

Conditions such as these resulted in textile worker organization as early as 1834, when 2000 female operatives struck in Lowell over a wage cut. Not until over 100 years later, however, was a successful national union launched with the Congress of Industrial Organization's establishment of the Textile Workers Organizing Committee [12].

In the nineteenth century, the efforts of labor organizations and labor reform advocates focused on the reduction of working hours and the removal of persons perceived to be particularly vulnerable to occupational hazards—children, but also in some cases women. The control of certain safety hazards by requiring machine guarding was legislated by state governments, but by and large management maintained effective control over the technology of production and its right to do so was seldom challenged.

Nevertheless, there were times when workers and their unions did mobilize over health issues. Our examination in Chapter Two of the campaign to ban the "Kiss of Death" suck shuttle in Massachusetts mills during the early years of the twentieth century suggests that byssinosis was a problem in the New England textile industry, but was masked by ubiquitous ill health—particularly tuberculosis—among mill operatives at the time. The dust diseases of mill workers were submerged in the contemporary scientific enthusiasm for germs and the public health science focus on anti-tuberculosis campaigns. For their part, organized labor and social movements concerned with work conditions used what science was available to them—workers must always rely on experts to diagnose and define their maladies—to successfully press for public attention to and legislative action on mill conditions. Their efforts were aided by support for the ban by a portion of the mill industry and the textile equipment manufacturing industry.

While the suck shuttle ban may have been guided by the wrong science (the suck shuttle did not cause TB), the important point is that the coalition behind the ban was responsible for one of the earliest attempts in the United States to regulate occupational disease.

Where the struggles over health in the mills in New England might have gone can never be known, for with the decline of New England textiles and the industry's growth in the South—our topic in Chapter 3—brown lung became a Southern disease. And, as textile unionism was never able to gain a substantial foothold in the South (the move South also devastated union strength in the North), the history of byssinosis becomes a tale of the relationship among science, business, and government rather than a study in labor history. Labor unions would not again play an important role in the story of brown lung until the late 1960s.

As mill owners established their power in the South, their control of both society and government became nearly all pervasive. Mill workers were considered to be the lowest class of whites, and were completely dependent on the good will of the mill owners for their economic survival. Within such conditions, then, mill workers lacked even rudimentary social, political, or economic power.

In the Southern states where textiles was the dominant, if not the only, industry, mill owners also enjoyed a great deal of control over government. Mill owners insisted that mill work was healthy and safe and that as outrageous a thing as workplace inspections were not needed. Few dared contradict them.

Still, industrial hygiene activity did go on at the state level. Our analysis of this activity in Chapter 4—where we focus on the work of M. F. Trice in North Carolina and James Hammond in South Carolina—suggests that in the 1940s cotton mill workers' lung diseases remained ill-defined, but enough was known about cotton dust hazards so that government agencies and industry might have begun preventive activity. Yet industry insisted, because of the superior conditions of the mills here, that byssinosis did not exist in the United States, though of course there was no serious study to determine if in fact conditions were different in the United States than in Great Britain. Appropriate government action, as viewed by North Carolina health officials, was to alert the industry to the cotton dust hazard and the British experience, and hope for the best. Industry's failure to act at this time cannot be rationalized on the basis that it had not been warned about the problem. Yet the cautious nature and overall ineffectuality of state industrial hygiene programs—with their emphasis on providing information and voluntary industry compliance—is of note here as well.

Complaints from mill workers in the Carolinas did result in a cursory review of cotton mill conditions by Phillip Drinker of the Harvard School of Public Health. In this review, Drinker gave the textile industry a relatively clean bill of health, and he viewed dust hazards in cotton textiles as minor when compared to the toxic exposures he had studied in other industries. Still, Hammond was intrigued enough by the possibilities of doing engineering studies of ventilation in the mills to solicit money from the industry and put together a research team. The work of this "Harvard Cotton Dust Project," which we examine in Chapter 5, resulted in the publication of a number of papers in respected journals. References in these papers to the possibility of byssinosis in the mills were, however, few and vague. The Project had little if any influence on the actions and attitudes of mill owners.

The Harvard Cotton Dust Project petered out in the early 1950s as key researchers moved on to other, more challenging questions, but conditions in cotton textile plants continued to generate dust-related disease. While little was being written or published about byssinosis in scientific journals at this time, representatives of Liberty Mutual Insurance Company, the major workers' compensation carrier for the textile industry, were both aware of and concerned about the problem. The company's involvement in the issue was not public knowledge, however, and while it had gathered sufficient information to warrant further, extensive investigation, the constraints of business confidentiality resulted in ostrich-like behavior by Liberty Mutual: the industry did not want to know that it had a serious problem and the insurance carrier would not bring in outside investigators without client permission. The presumed preventative purposes of workers' compensation were being subverted by economic arrangements between the carrier and the insured. We explore this relationship in Chapter 6.

Georgia state public health officials had been alerted to the cotton dust problem through the warnings of concerned primary care physicians and by abortive contacts with Liberty Mutual. By the late 1950s, state investigators in cooperation with researchers at Emory University were trying— unsuccessfully—to convince mill owners to allow an epidemiological study in their industry. Despite repeated assurances by the researchers of great discretion, the Georgia Textile Manufacturers Association (GTMA), as we discuss in Chapter 7, did everything in its power to stymie these efforts. A relatively benign, cooperative, non-regulatory state agency was being viewed by industry representatives as a devious monster of government interference. The extreme nature of the GTMA's response must be understood, we feel, in the context of the rising tide of social change in the South led by the Civil Rights Movement and the threat this presented to the once unassailable position of the mill owners. Times, indeed, were changing.

The essays on Arend Bouhuys, Chapter 8, and Peter Schrag, Chapter 9, once again point out the difficulties of doing scientific investigation into occupational health in the context of the private control of the workplace. Bouhuys had to turn to the Atlanta Federal Penitentiary to find a mill he could study; Schrag was hamstrung by bureaucratic, professional, and political constraints until government and industry were able to find a formula for releasing his important epidemiological study of byssinosis. Government and industry seemed to have been spurred to action by Schrag's threat to go public, to release his findings to Ralph Nader, which he eventually did anyway. Both Schrag and Bouhuys were investigators of unusual perseverance, and were willing, in their own ways, to challenge the power of the mill owners and the conventions of their profession. They were also at work within a time in which corporate behavior in general and industry health and safety policies in particular were facing increasing public scrutiny and disapproval.

By 1969, the work of Arend Bouhuys had firmly established byssinosis as an American occupational disease. Though much remained to be studied and learned about brown lung, it was no longer reasonable to scientifically contest the existence of a cotton mill workers' lung problem in this country.

Scientific agreement does not necessarily mean industry compliance, and mill owners by and large persisted in their strategy of denial. Such a strategy became more and more problematic as the poor mill conditions became widely known and as a coalition of progressive forces along with a sympathetic federal government were moving toward the creation of OSHA. Something had to give, and that something was Burlington Industries, the leading textile manufacturer in the United States. From 1969 into the early 1970s, Burlington opened up its mills to large scale epidemiological studies, and when the results were made known, Burlington publicly acknowledged byssinosis was a disease of the mills and that it was caused by the inhalation of cotton dust. The industry had broken ranks. Why and how Burlington did what it did is the topic of Chapter 10.

CONCLUDING COMMENTS

The Cotton Dust Papers is a series of stories, based for the most part on primary sources: archives, interviews, and court papers. Sometimes these stories are connected, sometimes they are maddeningly disconnected as later researchers remained either unaware of or, less often, chose to ignore earlier investigations and findings. Taken as a whole, these stories attempt to disentangle the threads comprising the complex social fabric of occupational disease. We try to understand how hegemonic ideology and raw economic power conspired to keep byssinosis a more or less open secret for so long.

All books have a beginning and end. We choose to begin where a coalition of social forces made a significant impact on workplace health and choose to end where another coalition—similar but at the same time very different—finally brought a pernicious occupational disease to recognition.

By such choices, much is left out here that, arguably, might be included. We do not deal in any detailed way with the public dispute over byssinosis which developed as part of labor's effort to pass the Occupational Safety and Health Act of 1970. Nor do we recount the courageous fight of the Brown Lung Association during the 1970s and 1980s to win workers' compensation for victims of the disease. The book does not tell of the long battle in the 1970s of the Amalgamated Clothing and Textile Workers Union and its predecessor, the Textile Workers Union of America, to force OSHA to set a cotton dust standard and to enforce that standard. Finally, the book does not cover the international struggle for health and safety that emerged as U.S. textiles gave way to foreign competition starting in the mid 1970s.

The above were important sequelae of medical and industry recognition of brown lung. However, the recognition of work-related disease is the first step toward prevention, the first step toward the control of the hazards of the workplace. How this recognition fails to happen—and how it does happen—are thus matters of singular importance and merit close scrutiny.

We are trying to find out about a disease of poor workers, workers with low wages and weak unions who lived in mill towns dominated by mill owners. But this is not a book directly about these workers nor is it for them. This is a book for health professionals and policy makers, for those who are studying to make these endeavors their life's work, and for the interested lay public.

The workers in the dusty mills of the cotton textile industry depended on health professionals—as do most workers—for the protection of their health on the job, and for generations health professionals failed them. They did so unwittingly at times, and at times despite their best efforts, but fail them they did. What may be learned from the story of brown lung, then, is the critical importance of social and economic factors in keeping blinders, and binders, on the public, on science, on workers as regards occupational health and safety, and the sharp ethical problems for occupational health professionals that emerge from this setting.

At present in the United States, despite the existence of OSHA, approximately 16,000 workers are injured on the job daily; every day, 17 of these workers die. Another 135 workers die each day from occupational disease, from exposure to toxins and chemicals. And as new forms of work and work processes continue to emerge, so do new kinds of dangers [13]. The story of brown lung in the United States may be history, but what it has to tell about how occupational health is done in this country remains as relevant now as then.

The Cotton Dust Papers is not simply about neglect, nor about bad people. This book is a tale of insidious social arrangements—rules of the game—that cause real suffering.

ENDNOTES

1. Arend Bouhuys, J. B. Schoenberg, G. J. Beck, and R. S. F. Schilling, Epidemiology of Chronic Lung Disease in a Cotton Mill Community, *Lung, 154,* pp. 167-186, 1977.
2. OSHA Fact Sheet No. 95-23, "Cotton Dust."
3. OSHA Fact Sheet. See also, OSHA, Standard Number: 1910.1043, Cotton Dust.
4. The notion of occupational disease and injury as a social construction is not a new one. The classic statement on the topic is G. Rosen, *The History of Miners' Disease,* Schuman's, New York, 1943.
5. Charles Levenstein and John Wooding, De-Constructing Standards, Reconstructing Worker Health, in *Reclaiming the Environmental Debate: The Politics of Health in a Toxic Culture,* Richard Hofrichter (ed.), MIT Press, Cambridge, Massachusetts, 2000.
6. Charles Levenstein and Dominick Tuminaro, The Political Economy of Health and Disease, *New Solutions: A Journal of Environmental and Public Health Policy, 2:*1, pp. 25-34, 1992.
7. Charles Levenstein and John Wooding, *The Point of Production,* Guilford Press, New York, 1999.
8. Daniel Berman, *Death on the Job: Occupational Health and Safety Struggles in the United States,* Monthly Review Press, New York, 1978.
9. Charles Noble, *Liberalism at Work,* Temple University Press, Philadelphia, p. 22, 1986. It should also be noted that altruism can take many forms. Southern mill owners professed a great deal of concern for their workers, albeit in highly paternalistic terms. Such paternalism proved a strong, or convenient, ideological barrier to owners

accepting outside investigation of byssinosis in their mills and—from their view—interfering in the lives of "their people."

10. Edward H. Beardsley, *A History of Neglect: Health Care for Blacks and Mill Workers in the Twentieth-Century South,* University of Tennessee Press, Knoxville, Chapter 9, 1987.

11. Pennsylvania Senate Journal, 1837-38, Part 2, p. 289. Cited in Anthony F. C. Wallace, *Rockdale,* W. W. Norton and Co., New York, 1978.

12. Joseph Y. Garrison, Textile Workers Union of America, in *Labor Unions,* Gary M. Fink (ed.), Greenwood Press, Westport, Connecticut, p. 383, 1977.

13. For the sources of these figures, see [7, p. 11].

CHAPTER 2

"Kiss of Death":
Banning the Suction Shuttle
in Massachusetts

A turn-of-the century weaver had to mouth her loom's shuttle.

The shuttle was the device that held the filling yarn and carried it across the loom to interlace filling with warp yarn. The weaver constantly had to rethread the shuttle by placing her mouth over the "eye" of the shuttle and sucking the filling yarn through; this was called "shuttle kissing." "In a cotton mill of plain goods and medium numbers, a weaver threads the shuttle of one loom about 100 times per day" [1]. That same weaver might tend six or eight looms at a time, repeating the shuttle sucking over and over again. If the weaver was out on any day, another took her place at her looms. In 1911, the Massachusetts legislature banned the suck shuttle on weaving looms.

The early 1900s had seen the development of a sizable public health movement, given vigor by the new understanding of the communicability of disease and focusing much of its energy on anti-tuberculosis activities. The impetus behind the ban, then, was the fear that, since more than one weaver often used the same shuttle, shuttle kissing would transmit infectious disease, particularly TB, the health scourge of the time.

In an era of sparse government regulation of production methods, Massachusetts' prohibition of the suck shuttle stands out as a prominent exception. It was among the earliest examples of attempts to regulate occupational disease in the United States. The ban of the suck shuttle ultimately resulted from the convergence of certain historical forces. How it happened, and why it happened in Massachusetts at that time rather than in another time and place, are the topics of this chapter.

In part, the ban came about because labor had secured legitimacy for its workplace efforts by presenting problems in terms that scientific and medical expertise had established as acceptable. Even though extremely dusty conditions

15

prevailed in mills at the time, it was the suck shuttle and TB, rather than cotton dust and byssinosis, that were recognized as the paramount health problems for the more than 100,000 Massachusetts cotton mill workers. It was TB, more than anything else, that was listed under "Cause of Death" in death record after death record filed in the municipal offices of New England mill towns. The ubiquity of TB, however, masked the existence, and thus hindered the investigation, of other very real health problems among mill workers—among them, byssinosis. The historical irony is that while the banning of the suck shuttle represents one of the earliest attempts by government in the United States to regulate the production process, it was done for the wrong medical reasons.

THE DEBATE OVER THE SPREAD OF TB

By the early 1900s, there was both a scientific and medical community battling pulmonary tuberculosis. Though scientists and health specialists had long been confident that Robert Koch had discovered the tuberculosis bacillus, little progress had been made in understanding how the contagion spread or what affected the outcome of infection. Theories abounded, but the spread of the disease remained a matter of speculation. Since there was no way to destroy the bacillus after infection, prevention of TB focused on suppressing contagion or increasing resistance. Disagreement raged into the 1920s about specific methods for effective disease control and their optimal combinations. These disagreements centered primarily on environmentally oriented measures versus personal care.

After discovering the TB bacillus, Koch and others learned that it maintained its viability as an organism for up to several months in a dry state. When the dry bacilli were injected into animals, the animals came down with TB. Koch and his associates believed that the infectious material was spread in sputum containing enormous quantities of spore-bearing bacilli. The transmission of the disease was, however, indirect. Koch thought that infection by inhalation of particles of sputum that were coughed or sneezed into the air by carriers was quite rare because he assumed such sputum was too large to remain suspended in air for very long. Koch argued, for more than forty years, that *dried* sputum broke into little bits that were carried and kept airborne in dust, thereby infecting people who contacted it [2].

Other scientists, most notably Charles Chapin, thought close and prolonged contact was necessary to produce infection and that the dreaded chance contact with TB bacilli in dust in the street rarely caused the disease. Chapin described numerous unsuccessful experiments to induce tuberculosis by inhaling dust containing live bacilli and more successful attempts to induce infection by exposure to inhalation of spray from consumptive patients who coughed and sneezed often. Many physicians, Chapin noted, believed that the lungs were not necessarily the primary seat of infection, and that infection frequently occurred through the alimentary canal—that is, by kissing or putting contaminated articles into the mouth [3].

Thus, from about 1890 to 1910, the health community witnessed two competing theories of TB transmission: one emphasizing the environmental medium spreading germs, the other focusing on close personal contact with an infected individual. The personal-contact theory was advocated under the banner of the "new" pubic health movement of the time, with Chapin as its leading figure, and was quite in line with this movement's emphasis on containment of contagious individuals [4].

In 1911, Chapin delivered a speech in Massachusetts exhorting people to, in the words of the alarmist headline in *The Boston Globe* (March 27, 1911), "Stop Kissing." Kissing, Chapin had warned, was "one of the most frequent methods by which dangerous diseases are transmitted." This admonition highlighted his emphasis on personal hygiene measures to prevent the spread of disease and his belief that oral contact with anything that came into contact with another individual should be restricted. That same year, Massachusetts passed a law requiring railroads to provide drinking water cups for each individual in every car of the trains.

Still, despite the influence of Chapin and the new public health movement, the issue of the transmission of TB—dust versus the drinking cup—remained unsettled, and it was dust that drew health officials through the factory gates.

INTO THE FACTORIES

In 1903, the Medical Officer of the New York Department of Health put out a circular that declared ". . . the keynote to the whole question of the prevention of diseases of the respiratory organs" was "the fundamental importance of the careless disposal of sputum." He hoped to

> . . . gradually inculcate the idea that the habit of spitting carelessly anywhere is not only filthy and indecent, but is in many instances to be regarded as almost criminal . . . [for] when these secretions are not properly destroyed at the time of their discharge from the body, they become more or less widely scattered, dried, pulverized, and suspended in the air as dust [5].

Ominously, it was called "infectious dust." And it was the dusty conditions in factories that led state health board officials to intrude into factory operations.

Factory health inspection began in Massachusetts in 1901. After the governor vetoed a bill on hours of labor for women and children, which organized labor had sought for three years, legislators responded to pressures from anti-tuberculosis activists and labor for measures to ensure that factories and jobs were more sanitary. The state Board of Health was authorized to begin factory health inspections to determine, in part, the conditions that promoted the spread of TB in workplaces and to make recommendations for prevention. The inspections would also help identify TB-afflicted minors so inspectors could also visit their homes to assess sanitary conditions. The Board explained how it defined its new duties which began in 1904:

> . . . it was decided to confine the inquiry chiefly to a number of those industries involving exposure to dust and to other substances of a poisonous nature. This selection was influenced mainly by the fact that the inhalation of dust predisposes to the development of diseases of the lungs, especially of pulmonary consumption, and by the additional fact that this danger can be obviated in large part by the observance of precautionary measures [6, p. xxiii].

In early 1907 the Board issued an important report on its activities in this area. The report described how irritating dusts affected the transmission of TB. First, constant irritation brought about "a condition of the mucous surfaces which more readily admits of invasion by specific germs"; second, the dust produces spitting and "promiscuous spitting" is "eminently unjust" as "those who maintain their homes in order and do everything needful to prevent the occupants from contracting consumption, therefore should be obliged to seek employment in factories where the most potent means of spreading consumption are allowed to exist." The dusty trades, therefore, led to an increased presence of "infectious dust" caused by dried sputum [7].

The textile industry was singled out because of its size and because vegetable dusts—as opposed to animal, metallic, and mineral dusts—were held to be the most irritating. Cotton dust, the report noted, may give rise "first to dryness of the throat and later to cough and expectoration" [7, pp. 13, 34].

The 1907 report was the first of five done yearly by physicians for the Board based on factory inspections. The initial report led to changes in the laws regulating factory conditions, specifically prohibiting spitting and requiring that factories be well-lighted, well-ventilated, and kept clean. District police had authority to enforce the law. Police inspectors were urged to take as industry standards the conditions in establishments using the same kind of materials where the "health, safety, and welfare of the working people are most completely protected" [7, pp. 3, 7-10]. This way of defining qualitative standards within prevailing industry conditions pervaded all health regulatory reasoning and resolved the issue of what could be established as "practicable."

The 1907 report also repudiated the suck shuttle as a "bad, unhygienic habit: since the weaver draws into her mouth fine lint and dust and if out for a day a spare hand substitutes" [7, p. 23].

Thus, if it was the scientific emphasis on the environmental medium which spread TB that led to the Board of Health's intrusion into the factory, the competing emphasis on personal contact with infected individuals created the climate for the suck shuttle ban. Politically, however, it was the fortuitous alliance between public health and organized labor that led to the ban.

LABOR, POLITICS, AND THE BAN

Trade union organization has never been a dominant force in the cotton textile industry, though it has varied in strength in different crafts in different locations at different times. In 1909, the cotton goods industry was the largest employer in Massachusetts with 108,315 workers. Although national membership of the United Textile Workers (UTW), including the affiliated Mule Spinners with a reported 2200 members, amounted to 9500 workers in the years 1909 to 1911, the total union membership in Fall River of affiliated and independent locals was 5000. Twenty percent of the textile workforce in both Fall River and New Bedford were unionized, and they were repeatedly and effectively able to mobilize non-union support during strikes. In all, organized labor in Massachusetts was a political force to be reckoned with, and working class voters were a significant constituency in textile towns like Fall River [8, 9].

In 1910, during the administration of Lieutenant-Governor Eben Sumner Draper, organized labor exerted enough pressure to force creation of a commission to investigate factory inspections; the commission's activities created a forum that made the suck shuttle a significant public issue.

Draper was well-known in textile circles. He was a leading member of the family that owned and managed Draper Corporation, which manufactured the automatic loom. He was also known for his conservative economic views:

> . . . he twice vetoed a bill providing for stricter enforcement of an eight-hour law for public employees, which action, combined with the fact that he employed only non-union labor on a 10-hour schedule in his own mills, won for him throughout his administration the active opposition of organized labor [10, p. 4356].

Nevertheless, it was on Draper's watch that the 1910 commission "To Investigate the Inspection of Factories and Workshops" was born, and one of its seats was awarded to John Golden, president of the UTW. Among labor's complaints were, first, the inadequate number of factory inspectors and their lack of training and, second, the dual authority for health inspections between the State Board of Health and the District Police which allowed the sanitation laws to go unenforced.

One of the first things the commission did was to schedule hearings, and they provided a platform for airing complaints about the dangers of the suck shuttle. Every trade union leader testified when the hearings were held in New Bedford and Fall River. A Fall River weaver named Charles Rafferty, who was also an inventor of shuttles, told the commissioners,

> The thing that puts everything else into insignificance in the textile industry relative to health is the suction of shuttles. Other things you can avoid by using natural means, the natural process of breathing; but when it comes to sucking shuttles, you have to suck them, and the construction of the shuttle is such that it needs a great deal of lung power to inhale the material that is colored,

sometimes it may be white, but in whatever condition it is, it contains a great proportion of dirt, poisonous material if it is dyed, and the operative who inhaled the substance is going to suffer more or less in health, and naturally in wealth, too, for he won't be able to follow his occupation as he would if he had a healthy occupation [11, p. 231].

Another Fall River weaver, Joseph Parks, described his experience:

I had occasion to work next to a man once who had tuberculosis. The man was continually loafing, he loafed about every Monday, he didn't take very good care of himself otherwise and ordinarily on a Monday he had what they call a "big head," and he used to be missing on Monday morning and a strange weaver had to go on those looms, and that weaver had to go through the process of sucking those shuttles all day long. It wasn't a very pleasant thing. I don't know whether the germs of consumption would be in the shuttle, but I suppose from a man having his mouth there continually that there must be some means of contagion.

I once had an experience myself. I went to work in a strange mill, and it happened to be a woman who had that particular set of looms, and before noontime I was sick. I was sick as a dog; I didn't know what was the matter with me, only I knew it came from the shuttles, I could tell from the taste of it. By morning my mouth was all broke out with sores [11, pp. 9-10].

Park's first anecdote might well be a description of a case of byssinosis; his second seems to describe the transmission of herpes. Rafferty is more concerned about the effects of inhaling dusts and poisons rather than developing TB.

The acting secretary of the State Board of Health and two inspectors also testified against the suck shuttle. All agreed the main danger was the transmission of disease, specifically tuberculosis, from using another weaver's shuttle. One inspector, a former weaver, explained that she and others had used sandpaper to clean any shuttles before using them. Both inspectors noted that suck shuttles were gradually beginning to be replaced [11, pp. 133-134, 323, 635-636].

It was a physician, however, who delivered the most impassioned testimony, telling the commissioners, "if there be in this whole State an instrument of greater destruction [than the suck shuttle], I do not know it. I believe that it is a curse . . ." Having surely gotten the attention of the audience, Dr. J. W. Coughlin continued:

I believe that no human lips can touch that wood that has become infected by the virus of tuberculosis without imparting it to the lips of a virgin constitution and ultimately impregnating that constitution and destroying that life; and I believe if those to whom I say this were up in the facts and believed them as I do, they would believe that every man who compelled its use ought to be execrated by every decent man who believes that every safeguard should be thrown around human life . . . Now I won't say that families have been disrupted by death by infection from this source, I have got no proof that this is so. Inferences are not facts, Mr. Chairman; and yet I have seen conditions that have led me to believe that death has come from the shuttle . . .

Mr. Chairman, when you say: You shall not drink from a cup in a public place, that there is a menace and danger in that cup to the public health, what must the danger be in that, where the weaver, wavering and tottering at her looms, whose life is almost on the verge of extinguishment, who goes home and died of tuberculosis and an innocent operative comes and sucks that shuttle to which her mouth or his mouth has been placed for months prior to the death of that previous operative, what must be the danger unless there is a resisting power to prevent that infection . . . the weaver puts her mouth up and shuts it down in her lips, and she takes, possibly, some of that dry material down into her lungs containing the fine virus it may be said to be in the most virulent state, which we know will cause death.

Now, this is a question not of fighting manufacturers; it is not a question of trying to start a revolution; it is not a question of trying to stir up strife between operatives and those who employ them, we don't want that...say that the State will insist that a safeguard will be thrown around those who use it and that the curse of the white plague at least will be driven from those homes which, to my knowledge, for 25 years have lost so many lives and the State so many valuable assets or shall no longer continue without a very vigorous protest from you gentlemen [11, pp. 259-260].

Without further questioning, the chairman abruptly and dramatically closed the hearing.

The person of Coughlin serves as a useful symbol of the social forces that influenced the suck shuttle ban: labor and labor reform; science, medicine, and the public health crusade against TB; politics.

A physician and prize-winning graduate of the 1885 class of Baltimore Medical College, Coughlin also became the first Irish American-born mayor of Fall River, elected in 1890 at the age of 29. Though his career ebbed and rose amid the internecine battles of Massachusetts political life, by the time he spoke to the 1910 commission he remained "one of Fall River's two best known Democrats." Conservative on financial matters, he was nonetheless seen as the Fall River machine politician with "a reform impulse," identified as generally pro-labor and an anti-monopoly defender of "the people" [12]. Still, other political personalities also played roles in the ultimate ban of the suck shuttle.

The following year, 1911, was a banner year for labor legislation. With organized labor support, Eugene Foss, a maverick Republican businessman who ran for governor as a Democrat, defeated Draper in the gubernatorial election. Although Foss did not live up to labor's expectations (twice, for instance, he vetoed a bill that would have allowed striking workers to picket and urge fellow workers to join in), still labor pressure on Foss and labor's influence in the state legislature allowed it to make substantial gains during his administration. Among the bills that became law under him were the 54-hour work week and the eight-hour work day, another on employer liability, and others establishing workers' compensation and a minimum wage commission. Jury trials were mandated by law in cases where strike injunctions were alleged to have been violated, something labor had long sought. Unionists also won the right to fine members for breach of discipline [13].

The bill to ban suck shuttles was introduced in January 1911 by Rep. Edward F. Harrington of Fall River who launched his long legislative career with the proposed law. Harrington was "following medical opposition to the old loom shuttle . . . to equip weave rooms with some type of shuttle that will obviate the use of the lips in threading," reported *The Boston Evening Transcript,* a conservative Republican newspaper, on January 11, 1911. It added that "anti-tubercular societies had the matter . . . presented to them some time ago and now Representative Harrington expects their aid in pushing the measure through the legislature."

After it was reported out of the Public Health Committee, the suck shuttle bill passed easily, one of labor's substantial victories that year and part of a remarkable, if brief, period of legislative gains by labor. Indeed, the chair of the state AFL legislative committee observed at the time that many legislators felt that organized labor had gotten "more than it had any right to expect in a generation, and that it should be content to wait more time before any further advance was made" [14, p. 39].

There remains one final player to be discussed in the move to ban the suck shuttle. The ban had passed, in part, because industry had not united against it. In fact, it is clear the manufacturers of automatic looms believed the issue could be turned to their advantage.

As early as 1908, the Draper Company, as noted above a major manufacturer of textile equipment, had drawn attention to the connection between the suck shuttle and TB in a newsletter called *Cotton Chats* that it distributed within the textile industry. After Massachusetts had passed a law requiring instruction about preventing TB in all public schools, and other bills on the prevention of TB, *Cotton Chats* reprinted an article about shuttle-kissing from an English labor newsletter. The Draper Company urged weavers to cooperate with mill owners in the "introduction of any device that will at so small an expense prolong their average term of life" [15]. Then, in February 1911, only weeks after Harrington had introduced his bill to ban the device, a whole issue of *Cotton Dust* was devoted to TB and the suck shuttle. The issue noted that,

> Certain trades or vocations have always been especially unfortunate in providing victims of consumption. Among such vocations, that of the weaver carries unusual risk in the process of threading the shuttles. In this process the mouth is applied to the eye of the shuttle and the filling is sucked through; generally it stops in the mouth but it sometimes goes further. The same shuttle is frequently threaded by different persons, affording ample opportunity to transfer germs of all kinds from one mouth to another. In a cotton mill of plain goods and medium numbers . . . an eight loom weaver would therefore perform the operation 800 times per day; in a year of 300 days this would be 240,000 times; or in round numbers over 200,000 chances per annum of inhaling germs of consumption [1].

Thus an important voice was added to the coalition advocating the suck shuttle ban, and this voice came from the textile industry itself. While we cannot rule out an altruistic concern for the health of weavers on the part of the Draper Company, the fact remains that in building a case against the suck shuttle, Draper was simultaneously encouraging a market for its product—the suck shuttle-free automatic loom.

Overall, the companies most supportive of the ban were those with the conditions closest to those that regulation sought to create; and, as we have noted, industrial health regulations were based on the best existing conditions. Usually, regulatory standards can be achieved by the vast majority of firms, but the amount of difficulty to achieve compliance will vary with the differing conditions and resources of each firm. For some, compliance will be relatively easy; for others, it will not be so simple. The very nature of enforcement of health standards led to divisions among the textile manufacturers. The firms with the best conditions often were allies in imposing the standards, thereby raising the costs for their competitors. It was a matter of capitalist economics.

THE ENFORCEMENT OF THE BAN AND THE ADOPTION OF NEW TECHNOLOGY [16]

The suck shuttle ban was made effective on May 1, 1912. Violations were to be punished by a fine of at least $50 for each offense. However, the law allowed an extension of the deadline for compliance if the firm "shall, in good faith, show . . . sufficient reason for its inability to comply" on time. And the Board of Health did grant two extensions, moving the compliance deadline to October 1, 1912. A few months later, when it was shown that "thousands of suck shuttles were in use in Massachusetts contrary to this statute," the board conferred with labor and management and again delayed enforcement of the law until January 1, 1915 [17].

As the time for compliance with the ban neared, *The Fall River Daily Globe* (November 21, 1914) trained its attention on the issue by reprinting an article from the English journal *Cotton Factory Times* which reported that Massachusetts firms still were not complying with the ban on the suck shuttle. The paper further noted that around 4,000 of 100,000 shuttles in New Bedford were of the "old type."

Enforcement of the law had been transferred to the State Board of Labor and Industries along with responsibility for factory inspections. That agency announced it would prosecute violators beginning in January 1915. True to its word, on January 14 Board Inspector Alfred Katz cited seven Fall River operations and eight New Bedford mills [18].

It would be convenient if the history of the suck shuttle ban could end here, but history is seldom cooperative. The fact is that the suck shuttle ban did not contribute to a general modernization of the textile industry in New England, and, especially relative to the South, the industry remained technologically backward. Ironically, the banned shuttle continued to be used longest where labor-backed political influence had been most adept at securing the ban in the first place: Fall River and New Bedford.

The suck shuttle ban had been instituted during a period when it was already being replaced by mechanical means. Indeed the existence of such technological innovation was a necessity for the ban, as Massachusetts lawmakers demanded evidence of a practical alternative before they would prohibit a production technique.

Before 1890, there were perhaps a half dozen patents relating to mechanizing the various tasks of the weaving process, and starting in 1888 the Draper Corporation invested $1 million to perfect the automatic loom, based on the breakthrough patents of the principal inventor James H. Northrop. This investment was the largest amount expended to develop a machine in the nineteenth century. By 1891 Northrop had developed the basic elements of the automatic loom and further technical refinements made it commercially available by the late 1890s. Yet marketing the new loom proved difficult in some regions, particularly in Southern Massachusetts.

Manufacturers in older textile centers in New England, particularly in the two largest Massachusetts textile towns of Fall River and New Bedford, were slower to adopt the Draper looms than newly expanding textile centers for rather obvious economic reasons. The choice between an old or new technology when equipping a new plant or addition is very different than the choice to *replace* an effectively operating machine with a new machine. Many of the factories in the South were just opening and being newly outfitted, whereas the New England manufacturers had capital tied up in massive amounts of equipment that, while not the latest vintage, still produced effectively. If in the South the decision was a matter of comparing the total costs of the automatic loom to its older competitors, New England manufacturers compared the operating, or variable, costs on their existing machines with the total costs of the Draper loom. Until the productivity gains and labor cost savings of the automatic loom were further improved, converting to the new loom simply did not make sense to many textile manufacturers in New England.

By 1914, 56 percent of the looms in the South were automatic, but only 29 percent in New England. Resistance to the new loom was concentrated in New Bedford and Fall River where the proportions of automatic looms were only 9 percent and 12 percent respectively while the two cities contained almost 40 percent of all looms in New England in 1914.

A second reason for the slow adoption of the new loom in these textile cities was their distinctive process for negotiating wage levels and thus labor costs. In Fall River, for example, local craft unions began in the mid-1890s to coordinate bargaining over the wage level with area employers' associations through a local Textile Council. The key to coordinating bargaining among occupations paid according to piece rates began with fixing a standard piece rate. The weavers' piece rate on standard print cloth was the key rate in negotiations between the Textile Council and the manufacturers' associations; negotiated percentage changes of this rate were then applied to rates for other crafts. The simple fact was that modernization would inevitably bring negotiations over the size of the increment accompanying increased output on more looms—manufacturers would attempt to reduce piece rates for weavers, and thus for other crafts, while the relatively strong unions and Textile Council would certainly resist such reductions. Manufacturers thus found their inability to unilaterally set wage rates a further disincentive to invest in the new and more productive Draper loom [19].

Significantly, however, not all firms joined in the manufacturers' "united front" against the automatic loom. Between 1909 and 1914, the Fall River Iron Works, which was no longer an iron producer and was the city's largest single employer with 20 percent of the city's textile workforce, made a substantial switch to Draper looms. The firm had operated outside the employers' association and did business right through a bitter strike that occurred in 1904. Unlike other Fall River mills, it continued to produce standard print cloth on a massive scale, had its own print shop, and operated at higher wages and lower costs than other local manufacturers [20]. It also was the first Fall River concern, and one of only a few local businesses, to relocate production to the South.

Other Fall River and New Bedford mills responded to the competition in standard cloth markets by utilizing the advantages of the more flexible, non-automatic looms for producing small runs of custom ordered cloth at lower cost. With lower labor costs Southern mills could produce standard cloth, but the less experienced workforce and distance from the Northern cloth merchants meant higher costs and slower delivery of highly varied, small production runs. The Fall River and New Bedford textile industries endured for as long as they did through a business strategy focused on niche production. This business strategy is the third reason for their slow adoption of the Draper loom.

Diversified cloth production also meant the necessity of minimizing costs associated with frequent production changes. As the less flexible automatic looms achieved cost advantages with longer production runs, the non-automatic loom—and thus the use of suck shuttles—persisted due to its lower cost and higher flexibility when operated by an experienced workforce producing small runs of varied cloth styles. Over time, automatic loom technology was sufficiently improved in its combination of higher productivity, adaptability, and less costly changeover to a wider range of cloth styles [21].

LESSONS FROM THE SUCK SHUTTLE BAN AND EARLY OCCUPATIONAL HEALTH REFORM

Use of the suck shuttle did not cause TB. Although many textile workers did suffer from "consumption," it now appears that the maladies of the weavers included symptoms of cotton dust-related lung disease—byssinosis. Whether the suck shuttle contributed to an increased risk of byssinosis simply is not known, we have found no indication that such a link has ever been investigated.

With the development of aerosol biology in the 1920s science was able to explain the transmission of tuberculosis. While Koch correctly identified that the tubercle bacilli cause TB and can be cultured from dust, he never learned that those bacilli in themselves constitute no TB hazard since their irregular shape and the electrostatic charge of attached dust particles prevent them from being carried beyond the protective mucous blanket of nose and throat. Bacilli in aerosolized large droplets produced during coughing, sneezing, and speaking are also caught in the mucociliary covering and cleaned from the lungs. It is the smaller droplets that may reach farther into the respiratory tract, beyond that protective mucous blanket, that spread TB.

Could physicians who saw cotton mill workers in the period roughly from 1890 to 1920 have had the necessary skills and diagnostic tools to distinguish tuberculosis from other acute and chronic lung diseases; would they even have known of byssinosis? Although in Britain in 1831 a researcher had noted the presence of a disease he called "spinner's phthisis" and in 1877 Adrien Proust had coined the term "byssinosis" to describe symptoms associated with exposure to cotton dust [22], there seems to have been no medical awareness of the malady in the United States. A review of the preeminent medical text of the period in question, Osler's *Textbook of Medicine* in its numerous editions, finds no reference to byssinosis, although considerable detail is given to tuberculosis in its various forms and presentations. Similarly, the prominent medical journals of the day—*New England Journal of Medicine, American Medical Journal, Journal of the American Medical Association*—emphasize tuberculosis and make no mention of cotton dust-related lung disease.

No doubt mill workers had byssinosis at the time, and workers contracting an occupational illness are of course aware of symptoms but may lack knowledge of their source and progression of the disease. Their interest in protection from work hazards may develop and acquire direction from public health education, and their organized pursuit of regulation may be in the context of health concerns acknowledged by experts in other contexts. Both situations were the case with the suck shuttle ban.

The suck shuttle ban is thus an early example of the enhanced power of physicians and other medical personnel as experts on issues of public health. Such power, according to a pioneering study by Samuel Baker, developed within the context of urban social conflicts and the increased demand for disinterested and knowledgeable experts to provide legitimacy for proposals put forward by contending social groups [23].

In the battles over TB and the suck shuttle ban, the public health scientists who emphasized the environmental influences on disease—like dust—were increasingly eclipsed by the physicians who stressed individual care and personal hygiene, although, as we have seen, both approaches were important to the eventual ban. It might be argued that had public health not gone in the direction it did—and why it did is beyond the purview of this work—byssinosis might have been "discovered" in the United States much earlier.

Be that as it may, it is nevertheless true that public health officials, physicians, and other health care professionals played a crucial role in the ban of the suck shuttle, even if, as was the case, the enforcement of the ban was never completely successful. But the role of such experts cannot be viewed in a vacuum.

The ban, one of the earliest attempts in the United States to regulate occupational disease and the production process, came about due to a convergence of historical and social forces, of which public health was just one. If public health and science set the stage by making TB a strong part of public consciousness, organized labor was central to leading this consciousness to a concern with factory sanitation and occupational health. In turn, the political attention paid to the suck shuttle in terms of hearings, inspections, and legislation reflected both a general preoccupation with TB and the specific political influence labor had in Massachusetts at the time. Public health entered the factory, and if only momentarily, both were changed: the link was made between work and health.

Finally, it is important to note that the broad coalition that advocated the suck shuttle ban faced a divided industrial community. Textile manufacturers were split between those who were already using the Draper loom (such as Fall River Iron Works) and those who weren't. Textile equipment manufacturers, most notably Draper, were anxious to expand sales of automatic looms and were politically influential; their support for the ban was surely of great importance. As we suggested in Chapter 1, in a country with an historically weak labor movement, fragmentation of the business class may be essential to the regulation of environmental hazards in the workplace.

Had the industry remained in New England, the subsequent history of occupational health in textiles perhaps might have been different. But the industry moved South, and textile workers in America had to wait another half century before the public health and labor movements and committed activists brought the health consequences of exposure to cotton dust to public attention and the regulatory agenda.

ENDNOTES

1. Draper Company, *Cotton Chats,* No. 100 (1911).
2. Robert Koch, Aetiology of Tuberculosis, *American Veterinary Review, XIII,* pp. 205-208, 1894.
3. Charles V. Chapin, *The State Control of Tuberculosis,* Fiske Fund Prize Dissertation, pp. 13-15, 1900.
4. James H. Cassedy, *Charles Chapin and the Public Health Movement,* Harvard University Press, Cambridge, 1962.

5. New York Department of Health, *Consumption is a Preventable and Curable Disease,* Circular No. 105, 1903.

6. *Annual Report of the Massachusetts Board of Health (ARMBH),* 1904.

7. *Annual Report of the Massachusetts Board of Health (ARMBH),* pp. 8, 13, 14, 28, 36, 1906.

8. George W. Coleman, Labor and the Labor Movement (1860-1930), in *Commonwealth History of Massachusetts,* Volume 5, Albert B. Hart (ed.), p. 446, 1930.

9. Martin Segal, *The Development of Collective Bargaining in the Cotton Textile Industry of Fall River and New Bedford,* unpublished memo, Baker Library, Harvard University, pp. 19-20, circa 1952.

10. Allen Johnson and Dumas Malone (eds.), *Dictionary of American Biography,* Volume V, Scribner, New York, 1946.

11. Massachusetts Commission to Investigate the Inspection of Factories and Workshops (MCIIFW), hearings, 1910.

12. Philip Silvia, *Religion, Politics and Labor in the City of the Dinner Pail,* unpublished Ph.D. thesis, Fordham University, pp. 721-741, 801, 819, 1973.

13. Richard M. Abrams, *Conservatism in a Progressive Era: Massachusetts Politics, 1900-1912,* Harvard University Press, Cambridge, p. 259, 1964.

14. American Federation of Labor, *Proceedings of Twenty-Seventh Annual Convention,* 1912.

15. Draper Company, *Cotton Chats,* No. 74, 1908.

16. For more detailed analysis of the process of replacing suck shuttle loom with automatic looms, see William Mass, *Technological Change and Industrial Relations in the Cotton Textile Industry: The Diffusion of Automatic Weaving in Britain and the United States,* unpublished Ph.D. thesis, Boston College, 1984.

17. Massachusetts State Board of Labor and Industries, *Second Annual Report,* Public Document No. 104, p. 31, January 1915.

18. Fall River Daily Globe, January 14, 1915.

19. J. T. Lincoln of the Fall River loom manufacturing firm of Kilburn, Lincoln and Co. later wrote of his experiences doing business during this period. He noted that radical modifications required in the long-established method of wage payments for weaving was a strong factor increasing the "selling expenses" of new looms. Cotton Textile Machinery—American Loom Builders, *Harvard Business Review, XII,* p. 102, 1933.

20. John Cumbler, *Continuity and Disruption: Working Class Community in Lynn and Fall River MA, 1880-1950,* unpublished Ph.D. thesis, University of Michigan, pp. 284-285, 1974.

21. William Mass, Mechanical and Organizational Innovation: The Drapers and the Automatic Loom, *Business History Review, 63,* pp. 912-917, Winter 1989.

22. See Robert E. Botsch, *Organizing the Breathless: Cotton Dust, Southern Politics, and the Brown Lung Association,* The University Press of Kentucky, Lexington, pp. 37-38, 1993.

23. Samuel Lee Baker, *Medical Licensing in America: An Early Liberal Reform,* Ph.D. thesis, Harvard University, 1977.

CHAPTER 3

Textiles Move South, 1920-1940

Three mill towns were the yardstick for the cotton textile industry in Massachusetts: Fall River, New Bedford, and Lowell, the city where cotton manufacture had first begun in the 1820s. As Table 1 indicates, production and employment grew rapidly over the years, reaching a peak in 1919, with a combined output value of $375 million and nearly 80,000 workers. These levels would never be reached again. Although production would remain relatively strong for the next few years, output fell drastically after 1925. In 1932, the cotton goods produced in the three cities were worth less than $50 million. Cotton textile manufacture had collapsed in New England. Figuratively and literally it went South.

Market analysts and social historians still debate the reasons why it happened—technological change, labor relations, regulation and taxation, wages, or various combinations of these factors. What is clear, however, is that the move to Dixie had important consequences for the recognition of byssinosis. While brown lung became a Southern disease, as strong as ever in a new workforce, trade unionism in textiles, labor's principal vehicle for airing its problems and improving working conditions, weakened dramatically in the move South. So, too, did labor's ability to influence state government. In the southern textile states it would be the employers, the mill owners, who would control government, keeping at bay "outsiders" and "troublemakers" who threatened their economic interests. For textile workers, this was a deadly combination of social forces. It meant that byssinosis would continue to sap the strength and the breath of mill hands, unrecognized and unchecked for another forty years.

WHY THE MOVE TO THE SOUTH?

Textile production came to Lowell, in part, for the abundant water power of the Merrimack River, on whose banks the town was built. A source of cheap power was very important to the manufacturing process, but a large supply of water was

Table 1. The Manufacture of Cotton Goods in Lowell, Fall River,
and New Bedford[a]

	Value of product in millions of dollars			Average number of wage earners employed		
	Lowell	Fall River	New Bedford	Lowell	Fall River	New Bedford
1875	16.8	20.2	2.8	9,960	14,216	1,983
1890	19.8	24.9	8.2	15,074	19,476	6,379
1899[b]	17.0	29.3	16.7	13,730	26,465	12,286
1909[b]	24.7	48.6	42.5	13,833	30,407	22,141
1914	23.0	50.0	51.8	13,066	30,758[b]	28,719
1919	60.4	135.8	177.1	12,479	31,805	35,206
1921	26.9	67.9	89.8	10,639	28,454	28,505
1923	39.0	100.9	120.5	11,683	30,774	31,955
1925	28.6	79.4	109.6	8,773	24,773	29,891
1927	18.9	66.7	93.5	6,758	25,552	29,079
1929	12.5	56.3	86.2	4,135	19,628	25,784
1931	4.7	27.6	43.0	2,391	13,255	17,702
1932	4.1	17.2	23.5	1,900	9,328	11,719
1933	6.3	26.3	36.2	2,488	13,638	17,027
1934	6.7	31.4	41.3	3,004	15,605	18,003
1935	7.3	31.6	33.4	3,059	13,047	13,091
1936	7.0	29.1	30.8	2,878	12,867	12,685

[a]*Census of Massachusetts,* 1875; *Census of the United States,* 1890, 1910, 1920; Commonwealth of Massachusetts, *Statistics of Manufactures,* 1914, 1919, 1921; Commonwealth of Massachusetts, "Census of Manufactures" (Mimeographed reports issued annually and separately for each city, 1931-36; each annual report reviews the immediately past ten-year period for the major industries).
[b]Cotton small wares included.

also needed for the dyeing and bleaching stages of textile production. Lowell also had an advantage in that the water it used was naturally soft, a requirement for many of the processes of textile production.

As Lowell's textile capacity grew, the railroads built sidings at every mill, the easier to move their product to market, especially to the demanding markets of New York City only two hundred miles or so away. And, finally, for years Lowell had reaped the benefits of a social structure that sent rural farm girls into its factories and its company-organized housing system, where they earned enough money through terribly hard work to either send home or lift themselves to a higher and more independent social status. Succeeding these girls at the looms and carding machines were the Irish and French-Canadian immigrants who thronged into the Eastern cities in the mid-nineteenth century, and the immigrant populations who arrived after them [1].

Power, water, transport, market, and workers. These, combined with Yankee ingenuity and Yankee capital, built Lowell and other New England towns into thriving textile centers. Textile manufacture did exist elsewhere; in the Southeast, for instance, it predated the Civil War. But for generations, no area could come near to the sheer size and volume of production of the textile industry in New England. Yet, as the twentieth century progressed, technological change was to enable a dramatic change in this equation.

As noted above, Lowell became a major textile center primarily due to the availability of water power. By the 1930s, however, cheap electricity had become widely available and had reduced the significance of water. As M. T. Parker noted in 1940 concerning Lowell,

> . . . the cost of power represents only a small percentage of the total cost of manufacture—about 2 to 3 per cent in an ordinary cotton mill; and it will therefore be much less significant than such an item as labor costs [2, pp. 125-126].

Nonetheless, electricity was just as available in the Southern Appalachian Piedmont and at comparable and even lower prices, thus enhancing the competitiveness of Southern industry [3, p. 99].

Water still remained necessary to the textile production process, and in Lowell, Merrimack River water remained relatively cheap. The expense compared favorably with Southern water costs which were as high as $1700 to $1800 a month. In the 1930s, though, the development of water softening systems allowed the textile industry more mobility, although at an increased expense [2, pp. 128-131].

Access to raw materials does not seem to have been a factor that seriously disadvantaged the North. In 1912, North Carolina imported about 25 percent of its cotton from other states, and by 1931 it was importing 70 percent. As the industry in the South grew, it produced finer grades of yarn that required a higher quality longer staple cotton not available in the Piedmont. Southern mills did perhaps have a slight advantage in the cost of raw materials, but Northern mill owners surveyed in the 1930s felt this was not a large or significant edge [2, pp. 131-136; 4].

Access to New York City was another matter. As the center of clothing production in the country at the time, it was *the* primary market for cotton goods. Simple geography gave Northern manufacturers a superior position. As Southern production grew, improving in quality and expanding in output, the region's manufacturers had to move into the New York market. Rail rates for cotton goods from Charlotte, North Carolina to New York were about 50 percent higher than from Lowell; combined rail and water transport rates were 90 percent higher [2, pp. 138-139]. The development of trucking and trucking networks, however, had a serious impact on transportation costs. The change was rapid and dramatic:

As the transmission of hydroelectric power has freed manufacturers from locations at the power sites, so the rapid development of trucking in recent years has freed them from dependence on railroads. Each of the present and former cotton mills of Lowell has its own railway siding; yet a cotton manufacturer reports that 99 percent of the finished products of his mill leave the plant by truck [2, pp. 148-149].

Thus while the North did not ignore the switch to trucking, neither did the South. And while geographically the North might still enjoy an advantage over the South in transportation costs, trucking surely significantly reduced that advantage, further increasing the South's competitiveness.

Widespread technological change, then, reduced the locational advantages of the North and made the cotton textile industry more geographically mobile. The development of electrical power, of water softening systems, and of the trucking industry established some of the conditions for a footloose industry. Yet these are enabling conditions, necessary but not sufficient to explain textile's move South. None of these conditions, alone or in combination, explain why a whole industry with massive amounts of capital investment would make such an exodus. Labor costs and the "business climate" of the South do. Again, M. T. Parker:

. . . [A] wide differential [in manufacturing costs] existed in the 1920's just preceding and at the time of the loss of a large part of Lowell's cotton industry. The cotton manufacturers consulted are unanimously of the opinion that the differences in manufacturing costs between Massachusetts and the South brought about by higher wages, shorter hours, and various legislative restrictions applying to labor in Massachusetts were a factor of first importance in Lowell's loss of industry [2, p. 163].

In 1924, when production fell dramatically in New England, wage rates for female spinners in Massachusetts were twice what the rates were in South Carolina. Weavers in Massachusetts were paid rates 63 percent above what a weaver made in South Carolina (see Table 2). While cotton textile workers in Massachusetts were relatively low paid compared to workers in other major industries—woolen and worsted goods, and boots and shoes—labor costs were 28 percent of the cost of textile production. This large a percentage made the difference in wages between North and South a paramount concern. Table 3 shows pay rates and weekly hours in 1924 for textile mills in New England and New York and in the Southern Piedmont. Wages in Massachusetts were nearly twice those of Alabama for comparable work. Looking at average earnings per hour for highly skilled work, New York's high ($0.541) was nearly twice what was paid in Alabama ($0.254), the lowest rate. Among those New England firms relocating to the South, the lower wage rates were clearly a strong motivating factor:

Table 2. Ratio of Hourly Wage Rates, Female Spinners and Weavers
in Cotton Industry, Massachusetts and South Carolina, 1890-1937[a]

Years	Spinners	Weavers
1890	3.03	1.92
1894	2.97	2.12
1898	2.73	2.08
1902	2.51	2.01
1906	1.54	1.58
1910	1.46	1.23
1914	1.42	1.29
1918	1.65	1.52
1920	1.29	1.17
1922	1.87	2.01
1924	2.00	1.63
1926	1.77	1.52
1928	1.47	1.46
1930	1.54	1.33
1932	1.74	1.28
1937	1.30	1.08

[a]Based on [2], Table 5, p. 162.

About that they were quite candid, at least within textile circles. When new England's Pacific Mills acquired a chain of South Carolina plants from Colonel Leroy Springs in 1923, the firm's representative pointed to "longer hours of work and a lower wage scale" as the main factors in his company's decision to move [5, p. 211].

Among the "legislative restrictions applying to labor" that rankled textile manufacturers were the 48-hour work week for women, enacted in 1920, and, oddly, legislation "governing the maintenance of firemen and elevator operators . . ." [2, p. 159]. Manufacturers also objected to Massachusetts' state income tax and, more importantly, to its corporate tax rates. In this regard, the South must have been looked upon with envy. In 1925, the "Massachusetts tax on cotton mills was forty per cent higher than in the Carolinas and sixty-six and two-thirds per cent higher than in Alabama and Georgia" [6, cited in 2, p. 171].

Enabling technology and cheap labor (plus the absence of unionization, which we will discuss) made the textile industry of the South more competitive and a more attractive area in which to invest. By 1929, the number of workers employed in making cotton goods in Lowell had fallen by almost two-thirds since 1923; in Fall River the decline was 36 percent, in New Bedford 20 percent (Table 1). The onset of the Great Depression was the final nail in the coffin. One of New England's primary industries was dead.

Table 3. Average Earnings and Hours in the Cotton-Goods
Industry in 1924[a]

	One-Week Pay Period[b]			Two-Week Pay Period		
	Average earnings per hour	Average full-time hours per pay period	Average full-time earnings per pay period	Average earnings per hour	Average full-time hours per pay period	Average full-time earnings per pay period
Massachusetts	$0.459	48.4	$22.22	$0.511	96.2	$49.16
Maine	.379	54.3	20.58	.496	97.1	53.62
New Hampshire	.458	54.0	24.73	.507	108.1	54.81
Rhode Island	.431	51.5	22.20	.530	103.3	54.75
Connecticut	.434	51.5	22.35	.496	101.1	50.15
New York	.450	49.6	22.32	.541	100.0	54.10
Alabama	.235	54.8	12.88	.254	114.4	29.06
Georgia	.252	56.3	14.19	.303	112.1	33.97
North Carolina	.311	55.5	17.26	.346	110.6	39.27
South Carolina	.253	55.1	13.94	.317	110.0	34.87

[a]A total of 114 establishments included in the survey. U.S. Bureau of Labor Statistics, Bulletin No. 371, p. 11.
[b]Hourly wages shown for the two-week pay period are higher than for the one-week pay period because all weavers were included in the two-week group and weaving is a relatively highly paid occupation.

THE COTTON MILL CAMPAIGN

When the War between the States broke out, the South was essentially an agrarian economy. Though cotton mills, as previously noted, had existed there nearly as long as in New England, they had not achieved significant size or status. Immediately after the war, as J. H. Street put it, the South was a "backward area." In a study of agricultural mechanization, Street compared the South to underdeveloped nations emerging from colonialism, summarizing the similarities of both:

1. An intense and highly specialized commercial exploitation of a basic extractive industry requiring little capital at the start, and utilizing abundant undeveloped resources in combination with large quantities of unskilled, routinized labor. . . .

2. The establishment of appropriate institutions of control within the region. The plantation system and chattel slavery succeeded by the sharecrop system, . . . bolstered by the local credit system.

3. Demographic characteristics of a predominantly rural culture which has begun to be affected by technologically more advanced areas.

4. A failure to make use of available technological alternatives to customary production methods [7, pp. 23 and 30-34].

The answer to the destruction of the old South and to rural underdevelopment, as W. J. Cash has discussed in his classic work *The Mind of the South,* was "progress" and the Cotton Mill Campaign: a concerted effort to establish a Southern cotton textile industry. The Raleigh, North Carolina *News and Observer* proclaimed in 1880:

> The South should . . . make money, build up its waste places, and thus force from the North that recognition of our work and dignity of character to which that people will always be blind unless they can see it through the medium of material strength [cited in 8, p. 190].

Thus, between 1880 and 1900 a modernizing "folk movement" (among whites) took hold in the South. In a region laid waste by civil war—"stripped of capital" according to Cash—more than 400 cotton mills were established. Gerald W. Johnson describes this remarkable populist crusade:

> Aspiring hamlets built cotton mills without any sort of investigations into the advantages of the locality for textile manufacturing. Only in rare instances was the enterprise headed by a man of any experience in business. . . . This was not a business but a social enterprise. Any profit that might accrue to the originators of the mill was but incidental; the main thing was the salvation of the decaying community, and especially the poor whites, who were in danger of being submerged altogether [cited in 8, pp. 184-185].

However shaky its foundations, these faltering beginnings gave rise to a Southern textile industry that by 1899 claimed a quarter of the looms in the United States. Twenty years later it had 40 percent of the looms. In the last decades of the nineteenth century, the Southern industry attracted ever larger investment, as described by Broadus Mitchell in 1921:

> Investments in Southern cotton mills increased about $2 million each decade after 1840 until that of 1870-1880 when the advance was roughly $6 million—from $11,088,315 to $17,375,897. The figures for the decade 1880-1890 reflect the suddenness and rapidity of the growth once the undertaking was entered upon; capital trebled to $53,821,303 and by 1900 had reached $124,596,879 [cited in 9, p. 232].

For all its inefficiencies, the Cotton Mill Campaign had been enormously successful.

To what extent, however, did Northern capital fuel this campaign? Contemporary sources in North and South Carolina insist the bulk of the investment was "native." This from Charleston's *News and Courier* (September 1, 1891):

> The great majority of cotton mills in the South represent the sacrifices and great efforts of the communities in which they are situated. In the East the cotton mill is built from the capital of the rich; in the South it is built from the combined capital of many of little means [cited in 9, p. 233].

True as this may be, Northern money also played a not insubstantial role. Northern money came ". . . from commission men, machinery makers and from manufacturers establishing plants in the cotton fields." The Yankee textile machinery manufacturers, anxious to promote their own sales, invested in Southern mills and quickly recovered their investments. Commission merchants (who engaged in moving textiles from the mill to market, extending credits, and working on commission) remained active as owners in Southern industry [9, pp. 240, 247].

Nevertheless, our rather cursory examination does seem to support the contention that the Cotton Mill Campaign, at least up until around the turn of the century, was by and large a populist, indigenous effort to establish a cotton textile industry that could compete with Yankee mills. And it succeeded beyond anyone's imagination.

By the beginning of the twentieth century, this regional development strategy had made cotton textile production the South's leading manufacturing industry. The Land of Cotton was also becoming the Land of Cotton Mills. By the 1920s, the Southern industry was presenting a strong challenge to Northern dominance, and during the early 1930s approximately one-third of Northern textile production closed down. Thereafter, the decline steadily continued:

> Cotton manufacturers from New England and the middle states transferred their operations to the South, acquiring and often extending existing Southern plants, or erecting new ones. During the transition, some larger firms maintained mills in two sections of the country, and some still do [1969], although the tendency has been to abandon the Northern locations entirely [9, p. vi].

What had been, then, a regional development strategy eventually resulted in—with the help of technological innovations and cheap labor—Southern domination of the cotton textile industry.

LABOR, TEXTILES, AND THE SOUTH

The shift of the cotton textile industry had drastic consequences for textile unions. Certainly there were unions in the South. The Knights of Labor had membership in every Southern state by 1886, and The American Federation of Labor was active before 1900 in Birmingham, New Orleans, Louisville, Paducah, and Dallas [10, pp. 24-25]. But as Table 4 indicates, labor activity in the textile industry was inconsequential compared with other parts of the country and even with other industries in the South. Ray Marshall notes that

> . . . relatively few strikes occurred in the South's leading manufacturing industry, cotton textiles. During the entire period between 1887 and 1905, there were only 32 cotton textile strikes involving 9,274 workers [10, p. 28].

The primary reason for the weakness of labor in the South was the power of the mill owners. As Southern industry flourished so did the mill owners. If the Cotton Mill Campaign had started and grown as a broad-based social movement, it ended up as the vehicle for recreating a Southern upper class:

> . . . by 1910 the barons and the stockholders of the mills were exhibiting a tendency to turn a smaller proportion of the total profits back to the building of more mills or the expansion of industry and business, in general, and to take more for their own purposes...Inevitably, the big showy houses made the drab cottages of the mill villages look drabber still [8, pp. 243-244].

At the same time, a new Southern lower class was being created. A necessary ingredient for the success of the Southern textile industry was a reliable and abundant supply of cheap white labor. This was to be found among failed farmers

Table 4. Strikes in the South and U.S., Total and Cotton Textiles, 1887-1905[a]

	Number of strikes	Percent South of U.S.	Number of strikers	Percent South of U.S.	Number of strikes S. Cotton textile percent of all South	Number of strikers S. Cotton textile percent of all South
1887-1894						
U.S. total	10,487	5.39	1,834,093	8.08	—	—
U.S. cotton	234	2.14	35,616	1.31	—	—
South cotton	5	—	468	—	0.89	0.32
1895-1900						
U.S. total	22,793	6.52	4,694,849	6.74	—	—
U.S. cotton	512	4.30	113,994	5.98	—	—
South cotton	22	—	6,819	—	1.48	2.16
1901-1905						
U.S. total	13,964	9.07	2,033,196	7.72	—	—
U.S. cotton	165	3.03	52,153	3.81	—	—
South cotton	5	—	1,987	—	0.39	1.27

[a]**Source:** [1, pp. 30-33, Table 1].

and other poor rural whites who came to the mills out of economic necessity. Yet, these newly born industrial workers were also seen by the mill owners and other "respectable" whites as a source of danger. Edward H. Beardsley explains:

> Although low, mean whites—"crackers" and "sandlappers"—had been objects of fear and contempt long before they transformed themselves into factory workers, mill laborers seemed a particular menace because they were concentrated in such large numbers and were so close at hand [5, p. 2; see also 11, especially the introduction].

Having regained a lost wealth, the mill owners were not about to lose it at the hands of mill workers. The key was control and the means of control was the mill village, dominated and more often than not owned by the company. Within such villages, as Robert E. Botsch writes, "The mills provided schools, churches, stores, and even their own currency. The goal of all these institutions was to exercise social and economic control" [12, p. 10]. Such power over the mill workers, not surprisingly, was used to stymie, by any means necessary, unionization efforts. J. Y. Garrison:

> Mill owners had absolute power over such workers and used that power to thwart any union activity. Suspected union members were evicted from their homes, set upon by mill-paid deputies, prevented from using the village meeting hall, hounded out of the village church, or jailed for trespassing [13, pp. 383-384].

Some years later, in the 1920s, labor nevertheless did begin to gain a toehold in the South, even while unionism was declining in the rest of the country. The AFL-affiliated United Textile Workers union (UTW) had lost more than two-thirds of its national membership, dropping to 30,000, in the years from 1920 to 1924. While it did not begin to recruit in the South until 1929, it was instrumental that year and the next, along with the more left-leaning National Textile Workers Union (NTWU), in spurring a wave of strikes in the Southern textile industry. Some actions were spontaneous, others were organized by the unions. Many of these strikes were crushed, often quite brutally, by the combined forces of industry and state and local government. A few of the spontaneous walkouts did garner some concessions from employers, but no permanent organizations were created [10, pp. 101-120].

Four years later, 450,000 workers struck across the country, including 170,000 in the South, in an action called by the UTW, which had grown stronger in part because of a friendlier political administration in Washington. The strike issues were union recognition, shorter hours, an end to work "stretch out" (increased worker tasks such as more looms to tend simultaneously), and an impartial arbitration board.

Despite impressive numbers, the strike failed. In many parts of the South, the strikers confronted strong counter actions. In both North and South Carolina the National Guard was called out. But "perhaps the strike was most forcefully suppressed in Georgia where Governor Eugene Talmadge declared martial law and had troops place strikers and their families in concentration camps surrounded by barbed wire." President Roosevelt later named a commission of inquiry, but little came of this. By 1937, the UTW still had only one written agreement with Southern industry (on this strike, see [10, pp. 166-169]; quote is from p. 167).

The UTW supported the creation of the Committee for Industrial Organization (CIO) and followed other industrial unions out of the craft-dominated AFL when the historic split occurred in the "house of labor." With the Hosiery Workers, the Amalgamated Clothing Workers, the International Ladies Garment Workers Union, the United Mine Workers, the United Rubber Workers, and the UTW, the CIO formed the Textile Workers Organizing Committee (TWOC) and in 1937 launched a Southern organizing campaign. As of 1939, 20 percent of the textile workers there had joined the TWOC, but this percentage is deceptive; a much smaller percentage actually paid dues and contracts were few. In Ray Marshall's words, "only 5 percent of the South's spindles were estimated to have been affected by union contracts, and a third of these were no longer in force by April 1939" [10, p. 171].

Soon after, the AFL was able to reorganize the UTW, while the TWOC became firmly established as the Textile Workers Union of America-CIO (TWUA). Whatever the organizational arrangements, however, as World War II began the Southern textile workforce remained overwhelmingly non-union.

In 1940, Great Britain, the other mammoth producer of textiles on the world stage, recognized byssinosis as an occupational disease and made it compensable. That same year the TWUA at its convention called for a

> . . . thorough study [to be] made of the hazards in the textile industry by the United States Health Bureau with a view of enactment of federal legislation which will eradicate hazards for both men and women in the industry, in so far as is possible [14].

In reality, however, sheer survival was the textile union's highest priority, and since a substantial portion of the industry was now in the South this meant survival in territory that could not be more hostile. Other matters, by default, simply would have to take second place.

Meanwhile, an obscure industrial hygienist in the South was becoming intrigued by respiratory "disturbances" among textile workers and started sounding alarms.

ENDNOTES

1. On the history of the textile industry in Lowell, see Arthur L. Eno (ed.), *Cotton Was King: A History of Lowell, Massachusetts,* New Hampshire Publishing Company and Lowell Historical Society, Lowell, 1976.

2. Margaret T. Parker, *Lowell: A Study of Industrial Development,* Kennikat Press, Port Washington, New York, 1940 and 1970.
3. B. F. Lembert, *The Textile Industry of the Southern Appalachian Piedmont,* University of North Carolina Press, Chapel Hill, 1933.
4. M. T. Copland, *The Cotton Manufacturing of the United States,* Harvard University Press, Cambridge, 1912.
5. Edward H. Beardsley, *A History of Neglect,* University of Tennessee Press, Knoxville, 1987.
6. R. M. Keir, *Manufacturing,* Ronald Press Co., New York, p. 350, 1928.
7. J. H. Street, *The New Revolution in the Cotton Economy,* University of North Carolina Press, Chapel Hill, 1957.
8. W. J. Cash, *The Mind of the South,* Doubleday Anchor, Garden City, 1954.
9. B. Mitchell, *The Rise of the Cotton Mills in the South,* Da Capo Press, New York, 1968.
10. F. R. Marshall, *Labor in the South,* Harvard University Press, Cambridge, 1967.
11. David L. Carlton, *Mill and Town in South Carolina, 1880-1920,* Louisiana State University Press, Baton Rouge, 1982.
12. Robert E. Botsch, *Organizing the Breathless: Cotton Dust, Southern Politics & The Brown Lung Association,* The University Press of Kentucky, Lexington, 1993.
13. J. Y. Garrison, Textile Workers Union of America, in *Labor Unions,* Gary M. Fink (ed.), Greenwood Press, Westport, Connecticut, 1977.
14. Textile Workers Union of America, *Proceedings,* 1941.

CHAPTER 4

Cotton Colic

A disabled cotton mill worker went before the North Carolina workers' compensation board in 1936. He told officials that his respiratory problems and fever resulted from the dust in the mill where he worked, and that his health problems were so bad that he could no longer work in the plant. A physician testifying at the hearing stated that he had treated 25 to 30 workers for the same ailment. The worker submitted to examinations by doctors and to x-rays. Nevertheless, the board denied his claim when the tests revealed no evidence of either silicosis or asbestosis, the only dust-related diseases for which the law allowed compensation at the time.

In 1938, the North Carolina Division of Industrial Hygiene had been called to another mill by local health officers to investigate workers' lung problems. There followed further reports of "respiratory disturbances" at local mills [1]. Clearly something was wrong, but what? Was this byssinosis? What was known about byssinosis in the United States in the 1940s? Could the textile industry state in 1940 (as it did 30 years later) that it had no knowledge of the problem? Could a responsible American textile manufacturer have been expected to know about the hazards of cotton dust in the 1940s? These are the questions that concern us in this chapter.

M. F. TRICE'S CAMPAIGN

M. F. Trice was an industrial hygienist for the North Carolina Department of Health and also the State Industrial Commission, its workers' compensation agency. Intrigued by the cases the Industrial Commission and Division of Industrial Hygiene were coming across, Trice did a review of the literature available on cotton mill illnesses and found a number of British studies. Chief among these was the work of C. Prausnitz, Britain's leading medical investigator into byssinosis. In addition to his definitive 1936 work on the topic, *Investigations in Respiratory Dust Diseases in Operatives in the Cotton Industry* [2], Trice also

41

came across Prausnitz's recommendations as presented in *The Lancet*. Prausnitz wrote that,

> The solution of the problem of [byssinosis] . . . lies in the complete removal of the dust from the atmosphere to which the workers are exposed. . . . Ventilation can do much but unfortunately even a powerful and well-directed ventilation will fail to act upon the lightest and smallest particles of dust, and it is these particles which have the greatest power of penetrating into the deeper portions of the lung. It is to the engineer rather than the medical man to whom we must look for aid, for there is no antidote for the persistent disregard of the physiological laws of the living [3, p. 267].

Trice became convinced by his research and by the cases noted above that cotton dust posed a serious threat to workers, and argued in 1940, in a short article in the trade journal *Textile World*, that "Effective dust control measures are essential" to eliminate the hazard. He was especially critical of the practice of cleaning or "blowing off" cards with compressed air which exacerbated the dust problem. While his recommendations focused on the cardroom, he also addressed the more general cotton dust hazard:

> To reduce the hazard, steps should be taken to control card-room dust in every mill in which it is present in excessive amounts. Better ventilation. . . . Use of vacuum strippers and grinders is recommended for all mills. Vacuum cleaners for general work should be used wherever possible. In some instances such improvements may practically eliminate the card-room dust hazard. In others, it may be that nothing short of complete enclosure and exhausting of cards will solve the problem.

Trice concluded by noting that all of the cases investigated by the state involved low-grade cotton. "No evidence has been obtained to indicate that any workers in these mills suffered any respiratory discomfort while cleaner material was processed" [1, p. 68].

Trice's article is quite remarkable. It seems to be one of the first articles by an American researcher linking cotton dust to byssinosis, though he was not allowed to use the word in the article [4, p. 232] and in reality—as we shall discuss later—he was confused over just what it was he had found. He also recommended extreme, for the time, and costly steps to remedy the problem in a journal widely read by mill owners and managers. Trice had sounded the warning and would continue to do so, but ultimately to little avail.

North Carolina in the 1930s was something of an anomaly in the Southern textile states where the power of that industry dominated politics, for it did, within limits, take industrial health and safety seriously. In the earlier part of the decade the state legislature had passed occupational disease laws covering silicosis and asbestosis. Enforcement and investigative powers were to be shared by the state's Department of Labor and a newly created State Industrial Commission, Trice's employer. In 1935, the state's efforts in the field of occupational health and safety were given a boost by Roosevelt's New Deal. As part of the Social Security Act, federal funds were made available for every state board of health to establish an industrial hygiene division; these funds sustained state programs until federal cutbacks following the Second World War. In North Carolina, this Industrial Hygiene Division of the State Department of Health, Trice's other employer, was to provide data and assistance to the State Industrial Commission.[1]

In the first five years of its work, the Industrial Hygiene Division focused on asbestos and silica related diseases. Approximately 10,500 workers had clinical examinations with chest x-rays. Studies of dust exposure were conducted in the asbestos textile industry, foundries, granite quarries, memorial making facilities, and in various mining activities. Significantly, textile mills were not a target industry for the Division except where asbestos was handled. Important as the studies of asbestosis and silicosis were, they tended to focus on industries that were of minor economic importance to the state and thus with little political influence. At the time, the textile industry in North Carolina employed 85 percent of all wage earners, yet, as a state study some years later conceded, from the 1930s to the 1960s only about 1 percent of state staff occupational health work had been devoted to the textile industry [5, p. 63, cited in 4, p. 218].

Still, to the credit of Trice and other state investigators, problems in the cotton mills were not entirely ignored. In a report prepared in 1940, for example, the Division reported health hazard evaluations involving "dust from low-grade cotton—bronchial and pulmonary trouble" and "objectionable atmospheric conditions" [6]. The State Department of Health itself was also seeing respiratory problems in textile workers at about this time. It prepared two reports on the textile industry between spring 1938 and spring 1939. One was devoted to card room dust problems, "the most pronounced effects of which are acute irritation of the respiratory system resulting sometimes in chronic bronchitis" [7]. And Trice continued to sound the alarm.

At a Safety Council meeting in Gastonia on October 27, 1939—among a series of public talks funded by the Department of Health on various industrial safety issues—Trice spoke on "Industrial Health—A Safety Factor" and reviewed the cotton dust problem. He reviewed a little known 1926-27 U.S. Public Health Service investigation of textile workers in Greenville, South Carolina:

> In a summary of the record of disabling sickness, 56 percent of the cases of illness occurring during the study were respiratory in nature . . . [though] The rates for tuberculosis, pneumonia, pleurisy etc., were very low. . . . For both night and day shifts the rates (for absences of two days and longer) for all causes were highest in the carding rooms . . .

---

[1] A useful summary of this organizational history, from which we have partially drawn, is to be found in [4, pp. 214-215].

The Public Health Service Researcher in the Greenville study had explained that card room workers "felt freer to be absent from work than those in other departments." Trice, however, dismissed this observation, noting that the illness rates in the card room were double those among spinners. He went on to discuss the cases of respiratory illness he had studied in North Carolina's cotton mills, and concluded that "All of the illness involving plant practices that have been discussed could have been eliminated or their incidence greatly reduced." As he had in the story for *Textile World,* Trice inveighed against the "blowing down" of machinery and urged that vacuum cleaners be used and local exhaust ventilation of machinery be applied more widely [8].

Over the next several years, cotton mill problems continued sporadically to attract the attention of the Department of Health. The Industrial Hygiene Division reported visits to do "dust counts" and to check ventilation systems, usually if the mill also handled asbestos [9]. In April 1941, Dr. T. F. Vestal, director of the Division, wrote to the U.S. Public Health Service for information about "mill sickness" [10]. At about the same time, Trice delivered a talk on "Occupational Disease Experiences in the Textile Industry" at the Division's 12th Annual Statewide Conference [11]. He also wrote "Cotton Colic," published in the industry journal *Textile Safety.*

The message of "Cotton Colic" was brief and urgent: "The evidence is overwhelming that cotton dust constitutes a very definite occupational disease hazard." He laid out his evidence. Cotton dust was recognized to cause acute and chronic disabilities among textile workers in Great Britain. Even in North Carolina, at least one mill superintendent had acknowledged the existence of "card room fever." Trice told of two incidents he had witnessed in North Carolina where workers had experienced "paroxysms of coughing...frequently accompanied by gastro-intestinal upset." North Carolina authorities as well as those in the U.S. Department of Agriculture had received similar complaints from mattress-making operations of the National Youth Administration.

Trice further reported that he had had an inquiry from an industrial hygiene engineer in "one of our western states" concerning a respiratory "disturbance" in a cotton mill. The problem in North Carolina and in the "western state" seemed to afflict only those who worked with low-grade cotton which was "yellow or tawny in color, and had a very definite odor." In Great Britain, he noted, a toxic protein had been identified in the search for a cause of cotton dust-related disease. Trice concluded his article by informing readers that the North Carolina Division of Industrial Hygiene would send a free bulletin about the problem upon request. The pamphlet included a digest of the British experience of the disease as well as a description of the North Carolina cases [12].

M. F. Trice was not a physician. It is now clear that he was describing not one disease, but two: "mill fever," which is an acute response to the biologically active material—fungi, bacteria—in contaminated cotton, and byssinosis, which is related to the component of cotton dust emanating, it is believed, from the endotoxins of the cotton plant itself. Trice did not, and probably technically could not have, separated out these two very different components, and so subsumed them under the term "trash."

But as an industrial hygienist, his focus on primary prevention was appropriate and reasonable, if perhaps naive: alert industry to the problem in cotton mills, sound the alarm. And this he did. In a speech to the Textile Section of the Statewide Safety Conference in Greensboro in May 1941, He said:

> Textile men may be the last people in the world to admit that occupational diseases are a problem . . . cotton is harmless—many mill owners will contend, however the experience in some mills refute the statement [13].

Trice nonetheless took an optimist's position on controlling the problem in the mills. He believed that combining efforts to bring about a ban on importing disease-producing low-grade cotton into the state along with education of producers would bring an end to "Cotton Colic." By linking the mill health problems with cotton dust and cotton dust to the need for effective ventilation techniques, and by spelling out the connection to industry, the mill owners would respond. He concluded his Greensboro speech by stating that "Probably by calling to the attention of textile men the existence of such possibilities there will be an alertness [to the problem]."

Years later, a colleague remembered Trice as a cantankerous old man who was hard to deal with. His optimist's glow had perhaps worn off, compromised by years of warnings that went unheeded. The Division continued to work on cotton dust problems, but no quick end to the issue was in sight. The office's monthly report for June 1941 said,

> More time has been spent in the investigations of outbreaks of acute illness among certain mattress workers in the state. This problem is in no sense completely solved, and further work is indicated. Cotton appears to be responsible . . . [14, p. 2].

WORLD WAR II

After 1940, the U.S. economy was running on an emergency basis. The ramifications of this industrial mobilization were significant for occupational disease, and for the government agencies responsible for industrial hygiene. In North Carolina in 1940, the Division of Industrial Hygiene requested additional personnel from the U.S. Public Health Service, offering the following rationale:

> The speeding up of the manufacturing processes had undoubtedly intensified the health problem. In those plants in which a potential health hazard existed, but which never became acute because the extent of the operations was never great enough to cause trouble, the health of the employees now probably will be endangered as a result of the increased tempo of operations [15].

The Division did remain active during the war years, including continued attention to cotton mill workers' health problems. In March 1942, one mill was visited for "special study" because of "poor ventilation and stuffiness" [16]. In July of the same year, the Cross Cotton Mill in Marion was visited to inspect the air cleaning system, and at Erwin Cotton Mills x-rays were taken of 746 employees as part of a larger Durham-based TB study [17]. But the war compromised the capacity to deal with industrial hygiene problems. A report of the inspection of Abernathy Manufacturing Company's cotton bag mill in Lainsburg in October 1943 gives a sense of the limitations within which the Division operated.

Steve Marsh, the inspecting engineer, was called to investigate outdoor pollution resulting from ventilation of the card room in a mill which employed about 75 people. A neighbor of the mill had been so inundated by lint and dust that the situation was creating health and fire hazards and "deplorable conditions." Marsh recommended that the owner, notwithstanding the prevailing "shortage of materials," build a "dust room" to control the problem and the owner was agreeable to the plan. Marsh also noted "very high concentrations of atmospheric dust in the card room which might be considered definite health hazards." (There is no record of any worker complaints or interviews with them, it should be noted.) Recommending improved ventilation, Marsh acknowledged that "Shortage of materials may also determine a manner in which this room can be made into a better place to work" [18].

It is quite evident, then, that the onset of World War II brought with it an intensification of occupational health problems and material shortages which would hamper addressing their solutions.

JAMES HAMMOND IN SOUTH CAROLINA

Beardsley succinctly sums up the status of efforts to protect workers in South Carolina into the mid-1930s: "South Carolina workers had no one to whom they could turn to protect them from dangers at work" [4, p. 214]. Factory inspection laws were in place but seldom enforced and the state legislature regularly blocked any attempts to improve or even investigate working conditions. The situation changed, somewhat, when federal funding allowed the creation of a Division of Industrial Hygiene also in South Carolina. With federal funding available, several studies revealed just how deplorable working conditions in fact were, especially in the cotton mills (see [4, pp. 214-216] for an overview of these studies).

In 1942, Dr. James W. Hammond was assigned by the U.S. Public Health Service to the South Carolina State Health Department to work on industrial hygiene [19]. A number of nurses who had worked for the textile companies told him they had seen many mill workers whose "asthma" had prematurely forced them out of the mills. Hammond visited with some of these mill hands, many of whom he found, as he described it, rocking listlessly on their front porches. These workers told Hammond that they thought their illness had something to do with dust in the mills. Hammond then closely interviewed superintendents and foremen and support staff in mills across the state.

Hammond's work was not formal research; it was not funded and he only pursued it when other demands of his assignment allowed. Still, his anecdotal store of information brought him to conclusions similar to those of Trice: somehow, something in cotton dust was making workers sick, and ventilation was important to rid the mill rooms of "noxious nuisance dust."

Hammond and his associate William G. Crosby, an industrial hygienist with whom he worked in 1947, looked at conditions in 5 to 10 mills in Columbia, Winnsboro, and perhaps in Spartanburg and Greenville. According to Crosby they checked dust levels, humidity, and temperature. Initially, Hammond suspected that contaminated water used in humidification was causing the trouble, but his investigations found the water used in the mills to be adequate. Eventually, he decided the cause of the mill workers' problems was to be found in the low-grade cotton that was contaminated with fungus, though he was never able, as with Trice, to separate the effect of biologically active substances from that of other components of cotton dust. Even with these inconclusive findings, Hammond urged improved ventilation where the opening, picking, and carding operations were conducted.

Hammond never wrote about these investigations for publication. He believed the work was too informal and neither "technical nor scientific enough," and he had neither the time nor inclination to do so. Hammond left South Carolina in 1947 and Crosby dropped the matter as he felt he did not have the "background" to continue the project. When a fire later consumed the archives of the South Carolina Department of Health, all records of Hammond's work literally went up in smoke.

Perhaps what is most intriguing about Hammond's work is that he does not remember ever having heard of others doing research on cotton dust at the time. While Hammond was conducting anecdotal investigations based on first-hand accounts from victims and industrial nurses, right next door Trice and the North Carolina Division of Industrial Hygiene were publishing alarms, making free reprints of articles on cotton dust available, speaking at safety conferences, inspecting cotton mills, spreading the word.

THE INDUSTRY

It is tempting to credit the 1935 creation of state divisions of industrial hygiene, particularly in North Carolina and to a lesser degree South Carolina, with accomplishing more than it actually did. At the end of the war, the fact remained that mill owners remained very much in charge both economically and politically. Division hygienists were no more able to circumvent or challenge that power than were any other state officials. In fact, Division officials would usually go out of their way to placate the prickly sensibilities of mill owners. North Carolina

Division head H. F. Easum stated in the "North Carolina Board of Health Biennial Report" for 1935-36 that his agency "has no police authority; it is purely a fact-finding organization," and that this "was probably advantageous in that the results of investigation will not be prejudiced in favor of either capital or labor. The intent . . . is to remain strictly neutral with respect to such interests" [cited in 4, p. 217]. Hammond, too, was well aware of who was in charge. As he later stated:

> It would not have been a wise and effective way to have attempted to be a policeman. . . . Conditions were set for you, and the terms on which the game had to be played. You had to play on the basis that the employer was the person responsible for the plant, and you had to work with him and his philosophy . . . [20, cited in 4, p. 217].

Still, the efforts of Trice, Hammond, and other investigators from the mid-1930s through the war years were not without effects. They seem to have been twofold. First, mill owners and managers were made aware of the disease byssinosis and of the possibility that it existed in U.S. mills. At the very least, owners and managers could not help but know something in cotton dust was making workers ill. Second, the well-being of mill workers, if it did not involve too much cost, became an issue for their employers in ways that had not been previously evident. This concern resulted from several factors: the bothersome information becoming more and more available on the wretched working conditions in the mills, the need to engage in public relations to counter such information, a labor shortage after the war, the need to meet the challenge of "Operation Dixie" (the TWUA's 1945 unionization push in the South), and finally the development of new technology and its promise of increasing productivity.

Industry response could take on an *ad hoc* quality, however, and often be remarkably obtuse. In 1941, for example, the textile magazine *Cotton* published a series of three articles by Erwin Hard on "Keeping the Mill Clean." The first article argued that cleanliness was important for high quality production and "builds good morale of employees, prevents fire and reduces accidents." No mention was made of a cotton dust health hazard. The second article recommended the practice of blowing off ceilings with compressed air, and the third suggested compressed air and a brush for loom cleaning [21]. These were, of course, the practices Trice had specifically and repeatedly warned against.

On ventilation, the industry seemed more responsive as at the time the development of air conditioning promised to solve certain production problems related to excessive heat and humidity and provide better working conditions as well. This from a 1943 issue of *Textile Age:*

> The mill of today must be air conditioned. In the opening and picking rooms, we would provide for recirculation, using filters for removal of lint and perhaps precipitation for extraction of dust. . . . In the carding, warping, winding and twisting departments, a complete system of air conditioning

would be installed, with facilities for distributing fully conditioned air to every nook and corner [22, p. 74].

Such visions of a postwar future, however, were not the reality of cotton mills in the mid- to late-1940s [23]. In March and April of 1944 a British delegation made up of industry and labor representatives toured U.S. mills and wrote an extensive report comparing the two nations' cotton textile industries. The delegation was impressed by U.S. technical superiority except in two areas: "fencing of machinery and dust removal over cards . . . are, however, probably inferior to those in British mills" [24].

The U.S. industry was generally pleased with the remarks by the British delegation, according to the *American Wool and Cotton Reporter,* but the journal offered a somewhat disingenuous defense of the dustiness of U.S. mills: U.S. cotton was dirtier.

> . . . there is so much waste in the bales other than cotton and…the cotton is so dirty that it requires about twice as much preparation to make the United States cotton suitable in yarn as it does for fiber produced in other parts of the world [25].

The industry was aware, then, that cotton dust was a real problem in the mills. While it might be argued that mill owners probably could not have been expected to make the link between cotton dust and byssinosis at this early date—Trice and Hammond were themselves, as we have noted, confused on this point—their knowledge of dangers in cotton dust and of extremely dusty conditions in the mills is undeniable. This should be kept in mind as we subsequently examine the obstructionism, prevarication, and denial of the industry in the face of mounting evidence of the connection between byssinosis and cotton dust.

There is also indication the industry was aware the problem of trash in cotton would become worse. At the November 1945 meeting of the Eastern Carolina Division of the Southern Textile Association, its chairman, Virgil McDowell of the Rosemary Manufacturing Company, issued this prescient challenge:

> In the future cotton will probably be picked by mechanical means, and consequently there will be more trash in it. What are you going to do or what do you expect to do to meet that condition when it comes? [25].

THE STORY SO FAR

In the Carolinas, by the end of World War II, cotton dust had been recognized as a likely health hazard, although there was confusion over the distinctions between "mill fever" and byssinosis. State officials had settled on improved ventilation, especially in the mill card rooms, as the way to remedy the problem. They also were familiar, certainly in North Carolina, with the British literature on byssinosis, and made serious efforts to notify industry about the disease and how to deal with it. During World War II, the cotton dust hazard became even more problematic and economic constraints interfered with the few efforts made to alleviate the situation. Industry response was minimal with no admission of the disease-causing nature of cotton dust, and compensation for such disease was simply not on the agenda.

The difference between the U.S. and British situation at this time is instructive. In the United States there was no organized protest over working conditions and no demand for compensation for afflicted mill workers as had been instituted in Great Britain in 1940. Union strength in the two societies explains much of the disparity. The war effort in Britain required that the large organized labor movement and its political party be included in broad political coalitions, and improved workers' compensation was one of the benefits of that participation. In the United States, labor representatives were also included on many war-related boards, but the unions of textile workers had been severely damaged and their agendas crippled during the textile industry's exodus to the South. Labor relations in the Carolinas allowed the industry owners and managers to pay scant attention to the workers' health problems.

In addition to the weakness of organized labor in the South—and unlike the banning of the suck shuttle episode in Massachusetts more than three decades earlier—there was no political coalition pressing for action, there was no general health problem for which the public demanded action, no medical community focused on finding a solution. All there really was were a few isolated and powerless industrial hygienists, responsibly and—given their time and place—courageously sounding an alarm to which few responded.

Meanwhile, the victims sat quietly rocking on the porches of their cottages, perhaps listening to the war news on the radio, and softly sharing their stories with the doctor or nurse or any passerby who stopped to inquire how they were. In their stories, they blamed the choking cotton dust.

*   *   *

In the mid-1940s, some worker complaints did manage to make their way to the Labor Commissioners of both Carolinas, and the U.S. Public Health Service was asked to investigate. The USPH hired Phillip Drinker, of Harvard University's industrial hygiene program, to survey "atmospheric conditions" in the cotton mills.

ENDNOTES

1. These incidences were reported by M. F. Trice in his article "Card Room Fever," *Textile World,* March 1940.
2. C. Prausnitz, *Investigations on Respiratory Dust Diseases in Operatives in the Cotton Industry,* Medical Research Council, Special Report Series No. 212, H. M. Stationery Office, London, 1936.

3. "Respiratory Disease in the Cotton Industry," *Lancet,* August 1, 1936.
4. According to Beardsley in *A History of Neglect,* University of Tennessee Press, Knoxville, 1987.
5. North Carolina Board of Health, *Biennial Report,* 1964-1966.
6. North Carolina Archives, Division of Industrial Hygiene, *Accomplishments as of December 31, 1940,* no date. Much of the following information in this chapter derives from materials in the State of North Carolina Archives. Notes will state "Archives" to indicate this source.
7. North Carolina State Department of Health, *Annual Report,* p. 3, May 1, 1938-April 30, 1939.
8. M. F. Trice, *Industrial Health—A Safety Factor,* Safety Council Meeting, Gastonia, October 27, 1939, typescript. Archives.
9. North Carolina State Department of Health, *Annual Report,* May 1, 1940-April 30, 1941. Archives.
10. Division of Industrial Hygiene, *Monthly Report,* April 1941, typescript. Archives.
11. Division of Industrial Hygiene, *Monthly Report,* pp. 2-3, May 1941, typescript. Archives.
12. M. F. Trice, Cotton Colic, *Textile Safety,* May 1941.
13. *Occupational Diseases Hazards Experiences,* presented to Textile Section, Twelfth Annual State Wide Safety Conference, Greensboro, May 17, 1941. Archives.
14. Division of Industrial Hygiene, *Monthly Report,* June 1941, typescript. Archives.
15. Division of Industrial Hygiene, November 1940, typescript. Archives.
16. Division of Industrial Hygiene, *Monthly Report,* March 1942. Archives.
17. Division of Industrial Hygiene, *Monthly Report,* July 1942. Archives.
18. Abernathy Manufacturing Company, *Inspection Report,* Lainsburg, North Carolina, October 20, 1943, Steve P. Marsh, Engineer. Archives.
19. Information on Hammond in this section is drawn primarily from two telephone interviews conducted by a staff member of the Southern Poverty Law Center, with James Hammond, August 17, 1983; with William Crosby, September 20, 1983.
20. 1979 interview with Hammond conducted by Beardsley.
21. Erwin Hard, Keeping the Mill Clean, *Cotton,* September, October, December 1941.
22. Simon T. Ellsworth, The Post War Textile Mill, *Textile Age,* September 1943.
23. By the late 1950s many, but by no means all, of the mills did have air conditioning. One impetus to this development was the introduction beginning in the late 1940s of textiles made of the synthetics rayon and nylon, both of which required precise temperature and humidity conditions in production [see 4, pp. 222-223]. Of course, workers producing rayon and nylon were not in danger of contracting brown lung anyway.
24. Ministry of Production, *Report of the Cotton Textile Mission to the United States of America March-April 1944,* HMSO, London, p. 22, 1944.
25. *American Wool and Cotton Reporter,* Vol. 59, 1945.

CHAPTER 5

The Harvard Cotton Dust Project

While Trice and Hammond were conducting their studies of the hazards of cotton dust during the 1940s, their efforts were overshadowed by another pressing problem: the excessive and oppressive heat and humidity of the mills. Cotton dust was certainly recognized as a problem by state authorities, TWUA, and by workers, but the fact was that the dust mostly affected only those who worked in specific areas such as the card room. Heat and humidity, on the other hand, affected everyone who worked in the mills.

Worker complaints to the state boards of health in North and South Carolina on working conditions in the mills had prompted both states to consider drafting textile industry health and safety codes, and both states turned to the federal government for guidance. It was in this context that in 1944 Verne L. Zimmer, Director of the Division of Labor Standards (DLS) of the U.S. Department of Labor, contacted Philip Drinker to do a "survey of atmospheric conditions in cotton textile mills" [1].

Drinker was an obvious choice for this project. He had done previous work for the Department of Labor, and so was known to Zimmer [2]. Although not an expert on heat and humidity, Drinker was a well-established chemical engineer turned industrial hygienist who had been on the Harvard faculty since 1922. He had co-authored two important books, *Industrial Medicine* with W. I. Clark in 1935 and *Industrial Dust* with T. Hatch in 1936. He had studied hazards in the rayon industry, and perhaps more importantly had done a considerable amount of work on the ship-building industry. Drinker was a pioneer in the engineering control of industrial hazards and much of his work had focused on the evaluation of respiratory protection, sampling methods for air contaminants, and ventilation control design. He knew dust and ventilation, and his interests certainly affected the direction of the cotton textile industry study he was to head.

In addition to being a distinguished Harvard professor, Drinker was also a Republican, a Presbyterian, and the product of an upper middle class upbringing.

While there is no evidence at all that Drinker's personal background had any bearing on his selection to head the mill study, this background no doubt did have a bearing on how he viewed the study. Having more in common with industry management than with the workers, Drinker seems to have seen himself rather like a private consultant, more concerned with the health of the industry that was being investigated than the health of the workers.

DRINKER'S INITIAL INVESTIGATION

The tendency of researchers to see a problem in light of their own expertise and to frame scientific questions from the basis of their own knowledge is a fundamental aspect of the scientific process. Occupational health and industrial hygiene are no different from other scientific work in this regard. In addition, these fields are applied sciences involving many disciplines, including engineering, chemistry, medicine, and toxicology. To evaluate the potential health hazards of an industry, all approaches to the problem should be utilized. Nevertheless, a scientist in this field who is asked to investigate a particular problem is likely to focus on the most familiar, more narrow discipline in which he or she originally was trained. This is especially the case if the investigation is hasty and superficial.

In the book *Industrial Dust,* Drinker and his co-author Hatch described two kinds of industrial surveys:

> There are two reasons for making dust surveys and appraising dust exposures. **Hygienic** surveys are made because it is known or suspected that exposures may be the cause of ill health, while **engineering** surveys are made to determine sources of dustiness and are then followed to check the effectiveness of remedial [action]. . . . Of the two, the hygienic survey is much the more difficult [3, pp. 113, 144].

The hygienic survey Drinker describes includes a medical study and a general sanitation study involving detailed evaluation of the nature of the dust exposure, general working conditions and ventilation, a determination of the distribution of workers by job, and an analysis of each job for turnover, absenteeism, mortality, and dust exposure. Yet, while Drinker had written classic descriptions of broad and comprehensive health and engineering surveys of industry, little of these methods were to be found in the report on the textile industry that he produced for Zimmer in June 1945—DLS Bulletin #18. The report was neither a full-fledged "hygienic survey" nor an "engineering survey" as he had described them. Half of the 16 pages of Drinker's report focused on the dust and lint problem and ventilation methods of control, while only three pages dealt with the main source of concern that prompted the study—temperature and humidity. This is understandable in light of his academic background and research interests, and might have been a hopeful step toward identifying byssinosis among textile workers, but no dust exposure measurements were reported and no medical study was done.

The report simply reviewed the general working conditions in the textile industry, and minimized the health problems of the textile workers:

> Studies by the Public Health Service have shown that the cotton industry is not an unhealthful one, and that it compares favorably with other industries such as steel. But a minor illness, cotton dust fever, is peculiar to the industry and has been known under a variety of names for years. It is not, however, a serious problem and is wholly preventable by means of dust control [1, p. 8].

There is no evidence in the report that Drinker ever talked to any workers, active or retired, as Trice and Hammond had done. He did, however, speak to mill management and related "cotton dust fever" to *their* work life: "This illness has been experienced by many mill executives to whom we talked" [1, p. 8].

Drinker's cavalier attitude toward "cotton dust fever" stands in marked contrast to his report to the DLS on welding he had completed a few years earlier. Here the danger was real. He wrote:

> There are definite hazards in welding, but as in other operations, the hazards may be controlled by adequate preventive measures. The typical health hazards associated with welding [include] . . . Illness caused by welding without adequate ventilation (e.g., metal fume fever, metal poisoning) [2, p. 1].

In the same bulletin, he had no hesitation in reporting the cause of "metal fume fever":

> [The] harmful substances generated in welding and cutting consist of gases and of microscopic particles in the form of fumes and smoke [2, p. 6].

In the cotton bulletin, Drinker compares cotton dust fever to the metal fume fever of welders:

> There seems to be a temporary resistance acquired by one or more attacks and lasting for a limited time. There is a comparable illness, metal fume fever, known to brass manufacturers and welders of galvanized iron, in which the resistance to a second exposure is measurable in terms of the leukocytosis (elevation in white blood cell count) which the illness always causes [1, p. 11].

Drinker's greater concern for, and scientific attention to, welding and shipyard hazards is peculiar. It may have reflected the nation's attention to the war effort at the time and the priorities this entailed; perhaps it illustrates Drinker's prejudice that only heavy manufacturing industries had serious health hazards. Whatever the case, one of the most preeminent and influential industrial hygienists in the country had given the cotton textile industry a clean bill of health. Also, Zimmer, head of a powerful federal agency, echoed and supported Drinker's findings. No alarms would be sounded here.

It is perhaps instructive to briefly describe the types of conditions Drinker would undoubtedly have encountered in the mills at that time. In the late 1970s,

Walter Jones, a retired mill worker stricken with byssinosis, testified before an OSHA hearing on establishing a cotton-dust standard. He said, in part,

> I worked as the clean-up man for many years. I used to do weekend cleaning. Every time there was clean-up weekends, I always went back and worked that shift. Then they started to giving us some of those little face masks, and we would use that. But they would get stopped up. That stuff would be banked up there, and it would be pouring down in lumps, and that mask wouldn't last long, so you couldn't breathe air through that. . . . The cotton on the floor, I'm telling you was six inches deep sometimes. The whole job that I done for thirty-five years was in the biggest of the dust. You couldn't see across the room. That's just the way it was [cited in 4, p. 61].

In the conclusion to his textile study Drinker painted a much brighter picture:

> . . . it should be recognized that health records in the cotton textile industry are good. There is nothing inherently unhealthful about the industry save for its tendency to allow somewhat dusty conditions in certain processes, and hot atmospheric conditions in others [1, p. 17].

Zimmer echoed Drinker's findings that there was no health problem in the cotton textile industry in his introduction to the study: "Unlike many American industries," he wrote, "the cotton mill processes a natural substance devoid of toxic risk" [1, p. III].

Despite his absolution of the textile industry, Drinker wished to continue research there. This may seem peculiar as he found the dust in the mills to be no particular hazard, but the textile industry afforded him the opportunity to pursue his real interest—ventilation controls. Here was an interesting engineering problem, and in the myopic way science may often work he betrayed no concern for the political, social, or simply human context within which this problem lay.

In his DSL report Drinker explained his reasoning:

> The practical mill operator has a fairly good idea where lint comes from in each process, but no one, so far as we can discover, has ever made actual determinations of lint generation . . . no engineer would attempt to install dust collectors in other industries without making such exploratory studies [1, p. 14].

Mill operators were resistant to his idea:

> Suggestions that such studies would be worthwhile were greeted with polite skepticism. . . . Mill managers to whom we talked about lint and dust collection questioned the practical possibilities of installing exhausts, even under looms, in order to collect lint [1, p. 14].

Drinker countered with an economic defense:

> Judging from results of similar programs in other industries, improvements of the type suggested will very likely result in improved working conditions and possibly in a reduction in the production of "seconds" [1, p. 16].

Apparently persuaded by his argument, or at least convinced they had nothing to lose, and reassured by his sterling defense of the healthful conditions of the textile industry, key companies involved in the industry agreed to his study.

THE HARVARD COTTON DUST PROJECT: BEGINNINGS

Following publication of the DLS report, Drinker began negotiations with the Nashua Manufacturing Company and Saco-Lowell Shops to fund research on the production and control of lint and dust in cotton textile plants. Nashua owned one of the mills Drinker had visited during his survey. Saco-Lowell was a major producer of textile equipment with whom he had consulted during his survey.

In September 1945, Drinker proposed a two-year study to the two companies:

> You supply the funds needed and we assign the work to one or possibly two students who would be working for a graduate degree in the School of Public Health or the Engineering School. Our Doctor Silverman would be an active participant and I would always be in close touch.

The study would involve dust and lint measurement from opening and picking through weaving. "We would determine what air flows are needed to collect and remove it continuously." Drinker asked for $10,000 for each year, half of which would go to salaries, $1500 for travel, and the balance for equipment. As always, Drinker was most careful in his proposal to state that he did

> ... not consider that the health hazards in the industry are at all important, but I believe that general working conditions could be greatly improved and the quality of the goods manufactured would probably be improved at the same time [5, Drinker to Edwards and Amory, 9/28/45].

The answer from the companies was prompt. Within two weeks, Saco-Lowell president D. F. Edwards wrote to Drinker that his company would contribute $5,000 per year for two years and that Nashua Manufacturing would do the same. "We will be prepared to cooperate with you whenever you are ready" [5, Edwards to Drinker, 10/5/45].

The only difficulty in the arrangements centered on the problem of patents for new equipment. Drinker assured the companies in his proposal that,

> if any new machinery or modifications of existing machinery are developed in the course of the work they would be yours. Patents could be taken out and assigned to you as they would be by members of your own organization.

Edwards found these terms agreeable, and wrote to Robert Amory, president of Nashua Manufacturing:

> It probably would be in order for us to get together soon and agree between ourselves how we want to handle any patents that might come out of this experimental program. With respect to this aspect of the matter I know you

will recognize our peculiar interest in patents by reason that we are machinery builders [5, Edwards to Amory, 10/5/45].

Within Saco-Lowell, top executives were uncertain about the possibilities for commercial development. Eugene C. Gwaltney, Vice-President and Director of Research, was a strong supporter of the project, arguing that,

> It will, at least, bring the issue of dust reduction in our manufacturing processes to something definite rather than the extremely general and indefinite measures we have of this issue. If certain standards could be set up, covering the amount and kind of dust allowable, we could approach the matter in developing equipment to produce this condition in a far more intellectual and accurate manner [5, Gwaltney to Kettley, 10/5/45].

Another executive commented:

> Although, at this time, I am not very enthusiastic as to the sales possibilities arising from this experiment, I am keenly alive to the fact that the amount is not great and the results might be decidedly worthwhile [5, Kettley to Edwards, 10/5/45].

Despite Drinker's assurances, however, problems arose when Harvard expressed concern to him about the relationship between the two companies and Drinker's research team. In November Edwards reiterated to Drinker his company's interests in the project:

> It is understood of course that we are engaged all the time in designing and improving textile machinery. Whenever, in the course of this work, we are able to design certain mechanical devices that are patentable we make applications for patents, and of course shall continue to do so with respect to any devices we might design for use in connection with the experiments you will conduct [5, Edwards to Drinker, 11/16/45].

In response, Drinker outlined Harvard's concerns:

> The university has a definite policy that
>
> 1. No patents shall be taken out by members of the university on subjects concerned with therapeutics or public health except by consent of the President and Fellows, and
> 2. No donor shall be allowed to receive special rights or benefits because of the money he gives to the institution.

Drinker attempted something of an end-run around these prohibitions. He reassured Edwards that there would be no competition for patents, saying, ". . . our study can [not] possibly result in anything of direct therapeutic value. . . . The cotton dust study is engineering and not medical." The Harvard researchers would limit their work to "analyzing and appraising conditions." "Designing machinery" would not be involved. Of course, the studies would be published, and if as a result any company used that work to design new equipment "that would not concern the University" [5, Drinker to Edwards, 11/19/45 and 11/23/45].

In light of the above, it is important to note that in his original proposal Drinker had outlined another key element of the agreement:

> Ultimate publication of results of the study would be undertaken by us and the University, your men helping in the preparation of the reports and approving the manuscripts.

Satisfied with the agreement, at the end of the month Edwards sent Drinker a check for $10,000. In December, Henry Wood, Jr., Deputy Treasurer of the University, accepted the company donations and expressed his regrets that ". . . there had been so much delay in getting this set up properly, but we trust now that things will move ahead promptly" [5, Woods to Edwards, 12/13/45].

Drinker's research interest in ventilation thus prompted him to pursue the textile industry for funding. Such a need for research funding and industry access, today and in the past, often plays an important part in shaping what research an occupational health/industrial hygiene research scientist pursues and how the research questions are framed. Here Drinker went to great pains to reassure the companies that his study would be "not medical" but engineering. While not surprising, given Drinker's oft repeated, though unsubstantiated, claim that there were no serious health hazards in the textile industry, this no doubt came as welcome news, especially to Nashua Manufacturing who had much to lose if medical problems among workers were found to be associated with mill operations. Drinker's arrangement on patents assuaged Saco-Lowell, and his giving in effect veto power to the companies over any manuscripts readied for publication was a serious compromise. Drinker's study was to be narrowly defined and strictly controlled; it hardly seemed likely to lead to the "discovery" of byssinosis in the mills, a disease that already had been compensable in Great Britain for five years.

THE STUDY

At this point, two other scientists entered the picture.

Leslie Silverman was trained in mechanical engineering (B.S. and M.S.) and in industrial hygiene (Sc.D.). As the cotton dust project began, he was an Associate Professor in industrial hygiene doing war-related research. In the past, Silverman had worked on Drinker's welding project. Part of his work had involved development of a new air-sampling method using filters and "gravimetric analysis" to replace the usual method of the time using a "standard impinger" and "electrostatic precipitator" approach. The textile project would give him more time and money and another industry in which to try out the method and perfect it.

The other researcher on the project was Frederick Viles. While a Lieutenant in the Navy, Viles had worked on the new air sampling method with Silverman for the welding studies. He had received an M.S. from Harvard in 1947 while working with Silverman as a Research Fellow in the Department of Industrial Hygiene.

Although, as noted earlier, Saco-Lowell's Director of Research, Gwaltney, was an enthusiastic supporter of the project, others in the firm, including Gwaltney's aide R. M. Jones, remained skeptical. President Edwards, writing to Jones while Gwaltney was away and just as the new project was getting started, commented:

> . . . we should examine rather carefully the means used by Harvard School of Public Health men for measuring the lint and dust content of the air. A simple accurate means of doing this would be very useful indeed. Of course, I know something of the methods now employed, but I wondered sometimes how completely the results of these methods can be made the basis for far-reaching conclusions as to remedial action [5, Edwards to Jones, 1/7/46].

Jones' reply was cautious and he seemed not particularly well-informed about the project:

> I do not know what means they use for sampling and it is unlikely . . . that Prof. Silverman know(s) much about the atmospheric requirements from a fiber-processing viewpoint. Unfortunately, fibers and personal comfort do not have the same viewpoint on atmospheric conditions, and what might be desirable from the standpoint of health and comfort of the operator might be ruinous to the processing of the fibers. Nevertheless, I am sure that with intelligent study, operating conditions can be improved both from the fiber and the personal angle [5, Jones to Edwards, 1/17/46].

Amidst such muted if nonetheless real disputes within Saco-Lowell, Silverman presented the first report from the cotton dust study before the Textile Section of the National Safety Congress in Chicago on October 8, 1946. Contrary to the spirit if not the letter of what had been agreed upon—technically, Drinker mentioned only publication—his paper was not done in collaboration with textile industry researchers, nor did Silverman submit it for company review before presenting it. Not until a month after the presentation was it circulated among Saco-Lowell's executives for comment. President Edwards first asked A. K. (Fritz) Landau in the company's Boston office to comment, and Landau was "not favorably impressed . . ." [5, Edwards to Gwaltney, 11/5/46]. Due to illness and hospitalization, Gwaltney did not respond until late January 1947. Since we do not have a copy of Landau's critique, we must rely on Gwaltney's response for a further sense of the controversy within the company.

1. Health Hazards

Silverman wrote that it was generally recognized that "the cotton industry is not unhealthful," but that "[t]wo occupational diseases of minor character may be attributed to exposure to air contaminants in cotton textiles." One he called mill fever or Monday fever, the other was byssinosis. Landau claimed never to have heard of a case of Monday fever. Gwaltney contradicted Landau:

> This [Monday fever] is just another name for mill fever and I am sorry to say that I have been a sufferer from this fever for the last 45 years, if I am out of the mills for any considerable length of time and then spend some time in the picker or card room.

Gwaltney also knew of byssinosis:

> While the disease . . . is rarely encountered in the mills today, in my early days, when I was an operative in the mill, I encountered a number of cases, the symptoms being like those in Mr. Silverman's paper [5, Gwaltney to Edwards, 1/21/47].

2. Machine-Picked Cotton

Silverman commented that Drinker's 1945 survey of cotton dust exposures in American mills indicated ". . . that dust and airborne lint contamination had increased greatly with accelerated production necessitated by war and reconversion requirements." In addition, he noted that the mechanization of cotton-picking, which was being introduced at the time, was likely to increase the "amount of dirt and trash carried with cotton . . . ," thus exacerbating the dust problem.

Countering Landau's disagreement, Gwaltney asserted that "the general consensus . . . of all cotton technologists [is] that machine-picked cotton will increase the amount of trash . . ." He went on to speculate, however, that

> the dust which is so troublesome may not be as great in machine-harvested cotton [because] the harvesting is done so rapidly after the cotton has been opened for picking that the dust storms will not have as much time to impregnate the cotton with dust as they would if the cotton lay in the field unpicked for a considerable length of time [5, Gwaltney to Edwards, 1/21/47].

3. Dust Levels

"Some of the figures [on dust levels] for different mill processes were rather surprising to me . . . ," Gwaltney commented, but he did not question their accuracy. "The device that they have developed for measuring dust content appears to be a very useful [one] and one that is badly needed in our future studies." From Gwaltney's comments there was apparent objection to Silverman using illustrations taken from the company bulletin, but he felt that ". . . when the opportunity affords itself . . . we will be able to extend the sale of our filter equipment if we use this report intelligently" [5, Gwaltney to Edwards, 1/21/47].

The discussion within Saco-Lowell did not seem to hamper Silverman's research effort, although he likely knew about the continuing skepticism of some company officials. In fact, Silverman published the paper he had presented in

Chicago in the *National Safety Council News* (April, 1947) along with a paper of similar purpose the same month in *Textile Industries*.

Interestingly, in his initial article, "Air Contamination in Cotton Textile Processes," Silverman reported on a visit to a U.S. Department of Agriculture cotton ginning laboratory in Mississippi that he made in order to determine ". . . why cotton cannot be cleaned more thoroughly in the ginning operations to reduce the amount of cleaning necessary in the textile mill." His explanation:

> In this country, ginning is a seasonal operation and cotton is ginned for approximately 65 days per year at the time cotton matures and is picked. A modern three- or four-stand gin will cost approximately $50,000 to $60,000 at the present time. To further clean the cotton and improve it one grade . . . requires equipment costing approximately $100,000. The increase in premium for this one grade improvement is not adequate to compensate for the additional expense.

Having already connected byssinosis to "air contaminants in textile mills" (though hardly unduly alarmed), and also having noted that the mechanization of cotton-picking was leading to dirtier cotton, here Silverman tied these problems directly to the economics of the industry:

> The majority of American gins are run by small operators or cooperatives, and the capital outlay required for the small return involved is not available or worthwhile. Mill operators must, therefore, be reconciled to the fact that ginning conditions will probably not change greatly in the near future [6, p. 26].

LABOR JUMPS IN

Drinker's original report for the DLS on atmospheric conditions in textile mills had been reviewed in the January 1946 issue of *Textile Labor*. Here, TWUA was quite militant, writing, "It is no news to workers that their working conditions are uncomfortable and unhealthful." The article named Cotton Mill Fever as a hazard and reported that some workers were so sensitive they had to leave their jobs. TWUA stated that although some industries had controlled their dust hazard, cotton mills had made few attempts to do so. The Union attacked the "callous indifference" of industry and suggested that industry's response to this and other health standards was long overdue [7].

By December of the same year, *Textile Labor*'s tone was quite different in a report titled "Harvard Battles Disease Common to Textile Workers":

> In experiments financed by the Nashua Manufacturing Co. and the Saco-Lowell shops, Harvard's School of Public Health is grappling with the problem of dust and lint control in cotton textile mills to protect workers from dangerous occupational diseases. Cotton textile workers are susceptible to mill fever and to a lung condition called byssinosis, brought about by long

exposure in the opening, picking and carding rooms. Byssinosis victims are unable to perform work requiring physical exertion. Now that the physicians have initially established the existence of the disease, the Harvard group, under Dr. Leslie Silverman's leadership, is experimenting with new exhaust ventilation systems to prevent it. Combined with an efficient air cleaning device, the ventilation system is designed to clear the air of dust and lint.

As far as TWUA was concerned, then, byssinosis had been recognized as a dangerous occupational disease, and so informed its members. The Union report was quite hopeful: science offered the promise of prevention. Indeed, just a few months later, the Union's Research Department reported that "the dust house is becoming an institution of the past . . . and . . . opening and picking rooms are becoming better places to work." Although, "the last word has not been said on reducing cotton dust," improvements in exhaust systems designed by studies at Harvard School of Public Health "hope to remove all dust hazards . . . and change radically the entire preliminary processing" [8].

One year later, in a similar report, TWUA's Research Department outlined specific machinery to be used in the removal of dust and lint, from vacuum stripping to exhaust hoods and general room air conditioning systems. The article noted the problems faced by users of these systems (for example, overhead cleaning without adequate exhaust) but reported about a mechanical cleaning system to deal with the problem. TWUA asked its membership to notify their local unions if their mills installed such systems [9].

These TWUA reports seem naïve and unrealistically optimistic. True, in his early reports Silverman had noted the presence of byssinosis in the mills but in the context of the mills being generally healthful and byssinosis being a "minor" ailment. The Cotton Dust Project was experimenting with new ventilation methods, but they were hardly being accepted as industry norms. The newest mills were somewhat healthier, but this was because of more widespread use of air conditioning. To say that the Project might remove all dust hazards was simply wrong. Why, then, the optimism?

The TWUA's purpose in the articles seems to have been political, at least according to the author of them, F. G. Bishop. In a 1986 interview he commented:

> My "On the Job" articles on mill conditions, describing the latest technology, and shiny new mills, were an attempt to stir up the workers in lousy old mills, and get under the skin of the mill owners. We also wanted to establish the deserved intellectual prestige for the union so that bargaining demands would be more presentable. If the mills were made out of marble and the machines were made out of gold . . . I would have found the need for more exotic alloys [10].

The effectiveness of such a political strategy, especially given the weakness of unions in Southern mills, is perhaps debatable.

THE REPORT OF THE SHIRLEY INSTITUTE

In the middle of 1948, Drinker informed his two funding sources that he wanted to meet with them to discuss the findings of the experimental project. He also requested that the unexpended funds—between $2500 and $3000—be used to send Silverman to England to visit the Shirley Institute and learn about British experiments with ventilation [5, Edwards to Gwaltney, 6/3/48]. Gwaltney and Robert Amory "agreed that it would be worthwhile to continue this work of Silverman's and Drinker's." Amory reported that he and Gwaltney liked the idea of sending Silverman to England ". . . to gather what information he could use on the same subject of measuring waste and lint in air. Also the maximum content of lint in air that would be agreeable to the workers" [5, Edwards to Drinker, 6/15/48]. Edwards agreed and Silverman went to England. In the Fall, Silverman wrote to Gwaltney about getting together to discuss the trip, but there is no record of such a meeting. In March 1949 Silverman honored Drinker's agreement with the funders by sending a draft of "Present English Practice in Cotton Textile Process Ventilation" [11]. He stated:

> I have been requested to publish this by the editor of *Heating and Ventilation* magazine. He has expressed an interest in wanting to make this information available to several people. If you have any objections, please let me know [5, Silverman to Gwaltney, 3/26/49].

Gwaltney was not available at the time and so his aide, H. J. Burnham, sent the draft to Edwards, asking him to communicate directly with Silverman. Burnham called Edwards' attention to only one item in the draft, that the "Shirley Institute is working on a 'sliver machine' to take the place of the card" [5, Burnham to Edwards, 3/30/49]. Edwards again asked Landau of the Saco-Lowell Boston office for comment.

Landau opposed publication of Silverman's article [5, Landau to Edwards, 4/4/49]. He listed five objections, first and foremost was that

> In my opinion the subject matter is based on information which rightfully belongs to the people who sponsored Mr. Silverman's trip to England. Since it is quite probable that the information he has obtained will be very useful to us when we undertake to improve our card the findings in this particular field should be restricted to our use.

Landau's second concern was to prevent the "general public" from learning that the Shirley Institute was working on a replacement for the card. "In as much as I have never seen even an inkling concerning this program in the journal of the Textile Institute, I do not believe that this new item should be released at this time." Landau also commented that, except for some minor items, ". . . the article is devoid of originality." He further pointed out a technical error and opined that few readers of *Heating and Ventilation* would be very interested in cotton mill problems. Finally, Landau commented that if the article were to be published, discussion of the "sliver-making machinery" should be omitted and no mention should be made of trip sponsorship by Saco-Lowell or of Amory.

Edwards spoke with Silverman "at some length about his report . . ." and other matters of mutual interest, including a filtering apparatus Silverman had developed for air sampling. Silverman agreed to delay publication until Gwaltney could review the article [5, Edwards to Burnham, 4/8/49]. Almost a month later, Silverman and Gwaltney still had not met, and because Gwaltney was traveling it seemed likely the planned conference would be further delayed.

In June 1949 the report appeared in *Heating and Ventilation,* so it seems that Silverman went ahead with publication without final approval from Saco-Lowell. He did, however, make changes in the article consistent with at least some of Saco-Lowell's concerns. He removed any reference to Saco-Lowell and Robert Amory (who by this time had moved on to become Vice President of Springs Mills). He did include mention of the new sliver machine, but softened this by revising a section critical of the inadequacy of ventilation of carding. In a rather disingenuous way he continued to minimize the danger of dust to the workers:

> Another important factor is the large machine to operator ratio. One operator can take care of 6 to 20 carding engines and therefore there are few workers exposed to card dusts in any given mill [12].

LABOR VERSUS THE ACADEMY

Having previously urged textile mills to install safeguards to protect the health of workers, TWUA set out in 1948 to influence state health boards to standardize and enforce safe atmospheric conditions in cotton mills. The Union produced a manual in which it informed workers and the general public how to determine whether air conditioning systems were needed in mills and cited surveys regarding the best temperature for efficient production. In this report, TWUA focused more on worker productivity as affected by dusty, hot conditions than on worker health [13].

The manual on air conditioning in textile mills was well received. *Textile Labor* reported that industrial, technical, and labor circles had been requesting copies. One response to the pamphlet by the president of an engineering firm stated that the "manual accurately sets forth temperature and humidity controls" and that "air conditioning was inevitable" and would bring increased profits [14].

When Saco-Lowell obtained a copy of the pamphlet, Edwards asked Gwaltney to call Silverman's attention to the publication [5, Edwards to Gwaltney, 10/13/48]. Gwaltney sent a copy to Silverman and Silverman replied in two days.

Silverman began his critique of the union report by indicating he had known about the report "for some time." Solomon Barkin, research director for TWUA and author of the pamphlet, had corresponded with Silverman eight months before, asking for Silverman's comments; Silverman was careful to point out, however, that he had ". . . had nothing to do with the preparation of the report." The Harvard professor had ". . . tried to point out to Mr. Barkin that many of the things he was proposing were ideal and that they had not necessarily been proved in practice." Silverman was also critical of the Union's "assumption that textile workers or shop foremen—that is, union members—are competent enough to make their own measurements of environmental conditions." In his experience, workers could not be expected "to be sufficiently familiar with technical details to make temperature and humidity surveys of this kind."

Perhaps most interesting, given that they had previously been somewhat at odds on the matter, was Silverman's warning to the Union about dust problems:

> I also tried to point out that they should say something about reducing dust conditions in mills, since I felt this was something which could be done quite easily and with available equipment, but they took no cognizance of my comments.

"Aside from its ideal aspects," Silverman concluded, "I believe the report may be of some value. It is questionable whether the Union people should be the ones to propose what type equipment should be installed" [5, Silverman to Gwaltney, 10/22/48].

Gwaltney forwarded Silverman's letter to Edwards with the comment, "The letter speaks for itself and will give you some idea of Silverman's capacity and judgment" [5, Gwaltney to Edwards, 11/1/48]. Edwards replied in a few days: "I like his letter because it suggests that he is a sound and thorough man who does not accept opinions of other people unless they are well supported by good factual evidence" [5, Edwards to Gwaltney, 11/4/48].

At the same time as Edwards was praising Silverman's character, the TWUA was struggling to win some protection for workers' health in Southern state legislatures. But the truth was that labor did not have enough political strength in the South to win its demands. Trade unions in cotton textiles could only hope to have some impact on industrial technology if workers' needs intersected with the agendas of others who were more powerful. Hence TWUA's emphasis on productivity in its manual on air conditioning in the mills—here was something it might win—and its disinclination at this point to push dust and workers' health. From his situation, Silverman could not have been expected to grasp this strategy.

Bills to standardize air quality in textile mills were introduced in South Carolina in 1948 and in Georgia in 1949. The *Southern Textile News* "blasted" the South Carolina legislature for even considering a bill to air condition the textile mills, and "accused law-makers of straying from the path of reason . . . air conditioning would hamstring . . . strangle . . . cripple the industry" [15]. After the lower house of the legislature actually passed the proposed legislation, employers organized a march on the state capital and succeeded in stopping the bill.

In Georgia, state legislators walked out of a hearing on proposed air conditioning legislation before a union technical representative could speak because they had been told that the union was run by a "Polish Communist" [10]. The legislators exited to attend an employer-funded barbecue, leaving the union speakers alone in the hearing room (apparently they were not invited to the barbecue). Georgia's General Assembly killed the bill after a few months of debate, citing the Cotton Manufacturers Association opposition.

THE QUIET END OF THE COTTON DUST PROJECT

A last article produced by the Cotton Dust Project was written by Silverman and Viles, entitled "The Determination of Cotton Textile Dusts in Air," and was published in the *Textile Research Journal,* February 1950 [16]. Silverman introduced the piece with a very strong statement about health effects:

> Our investigations have shown that there is a definite relationship between total concentration of contaminants in the atmosphere and the incidence of the acute disease [16, p. 110].

Silverman, ever cautious it seems, had been urged to strengthen his discussion of the health problem by the editor of the *Textile Research Journal,* Julian Jacobs. He wrote to him:

> I would like to suggest that the introduction be amplified in such a way as to emphasize the fact that dust in the opening rooms and preparatory processes in cotton mills is still a problem. It is my understanding that there are many mills who have not installed filters and other means of eliminating the dust hazard. Also, that respiratory ailments frequently causing fever are prevalent among those who strip the cards [17, Jacobs to Silverman, 8/16/49].

In a rare bit of candor, Silverman replied:

> As a matter of fact, it is only the exceptional mill rather than the usual which has attempted to adequately control dust exposures [17, Silverman to Jacobs, 8/26/49].

Through his studies, Silverman had apparently been brought to the view that byssinosis was indeed an American problem. He also was aware of a U.S. Public Health Service review of cotton dust research authored by B. H. Caminata and others. The review stated that "Mill fever and byssinosis have been generally associated with the cotton dust industry wherever it has been established" [18]. It went on to note, however, that there existed no studies in the United States that confirmed that view, and concluded:

> Investigation of dusts of plant origin from the standpoint of health hazard has hardly been initiated. This is emphatically true of cotton dust. There is need for engineering studies to determine degree of dust exposure and the factors governing dust production in the cotton industry, for complete data on the

chemical and physical properties of the dust, for compilation of mortality and morbidity data on cotton operatives and for experimental work on the mechanisms of the production of the various disease entities associated with the inhalation of cotton dust [18, p. 72].

Although such a study would have been consistent with the approach Drinker and Hatch had advocated in 1936, this is not what was done in the Harvard Cotton Dust Project.

By early 1950, the Harvard Cotton Dust Project was essentially over. In February 1950 Silverman wrote to a researcher at the British Cotton Industry Research Association that he would ". . . be delighted to have you come and discuss Cardroom dust problems. Actually we have not been working on this problem for the past year but are still interested" [17, Silverman to Charnley, 2/13/50]. The Cotton Dust Project researchers had moved on.

CONCLUSIONS

With all its convoluted history, what in the end did the Harvard Cotton Dust Project achieve? That is a difficult question to answer, as it depends on one's viewpoint.

For an academic, the outcome of greatest importance for any project is the publication of the results of the research. Despite the applied nature of occupational health and industrial hygiene research, the outcome of interest is not a verifiable change in working conditions but rather the identification of a health hazard and its parameters. It is deemed sufficient to disseminate this information in professional journals for use by government agencies, unions, and companies whose responsibility is the removal of the health hazards through their own work processes and channels. From this perspective, then, the Cotton Dust Project was successful in that it published six papers, plus Drinker's original report for DLS.

Drinker's report (1945) maintained there was no significant health problem in the industry, though no medical testing had been conducted [1]. He still held this position nine years later in a 1954 revised version of *Industrial Dust* [1, revised 1954].

Silverman wrote the second and third papers (April 1947) in which he cautiously acknowledged "a lung condition which is called byssinosis" and urged control of dust and airborne lint to eliminate it. He discussed the development of new equipment for sampling air contaminants, which was itself important work that moved the technology toward more portable methods that were easier to use. Silverman also reported the air levels of total dust and cellulose for 13 textile industry operations. The highest levels of total dust and cellulose were found in the operations preceding combing—opening, picking, carding, "slubbing," and "roving" the cotton. He then discussed control methods, including the drawbacks of several air-cleaning devices in use at the time.

Silverman and Viles collaborated on the fourth paper (October 1947) which delivered a mixed message on health problems in mills. They viewed cotton mill fever and byssinosis as "minor" problems, yet recommended ventilation for such reasons as reducing seconds and eliminating nuisance dust [19]. The fifth paper, also by Silverman and Viles, (1949) describes the chemical procedures developed to estimate the starch and cellulose, or cotton lint, in air samples in cotton textile plants [20].

Silverman alone wrote the next paper (June 1949) which was a report on his visit to England's Shirley Institute. He discussed the research being done at the Institute and explained the systems in use in some English textile factories. He noted byssinosis was a compensable disease in Britain and pointed out that it was because of byssinosis that the Institute had been asked to study ways to reduce card room dust levels.

The final paper, by Silverman and Viles (1950), most explicitly acknowledged the health hazard of cotton dust exposure. They cite Caminata and his co-authors on exposure to cotton dust as "an industrial problem of recognized importance." They continue:

> Our investigations have shown that there is a definite relationship between total concentration of contaminants in the atmosphere and the incidence of the acute disease. When the total concentration of contaminants in cotton cleaning operations is maintained below 5 mg/m3, it has been our experience that there are no complaints of irritation or fever. Undoubtedly, the incidence of the chronic disease is also related to concentration of contaminants in the air. In order to adequately control the health hazards, therefore, it is essential to have some knowledge of atmospheric contamination in the working environment [16, p. 110].

Clearly, Silverman had gradually moved to an acknowledgment of the existence of byssinosis and its association with exposure to cotton dust. Yet, how wide was the distribution of the research findings?

None of the journals was obscure, and some were directly aimed at the textile industry. The final article was published by the Textile Research Institute, an important source of information for the industry. The earlier papers also had wide currency. Requests for copies came from engineers designing textile plants in Greenville, South Carolina and from an industrial hygienist with the Department of Health in Georgia [21]. The chief of the Industrial Hygiene Division of Ohio's Department of Health wrote that he had seen the first report in *Heating and Ventilation* and was looking for the subsequent paper [21, Mancuso to Silverman, 4/27/49]. An industrial hygienist at Firestone Tire and Rubber Company wrote for reprints of the Shirley Institute Report [21, Mallette to Silverman, 8/2/49]. The research division of Chicopee Manufacturing Company, a New England textile manufacturer, wrote for reprints of the same article, noting the company was "intensely interested in the problem of dust control, particularly in the card room" [21, Griswold to Silverman, 7/29/49].

In the North and South, in industry and government agencies, the Harvard Cotton Dust Project had received serious attention; the academics' job of disseminating information had been completed. But the knowledge it had produced did not penetrate to other communities—the medical community for one—much as earlier knowledge had not crossed the Atlantic from Britain when that nation recognized and made compensable byssinosis. Knowledge generated by the Project by and large failed to take root even in the scientific community. Years later, other scientists faced protracted new battles to "discover" byssinosis in American workers. The Project did not produce a solution that changed conditions for mill workers.

Relations were complex among university scientists, industry, and labor in the cotton textile industry even before byssinosis or "brown lung" was recognized in the late 1970s. Focusing on the role of university researchers reveals how the pressures and ambiguities of their work environment affected the conduct of occupational health science.

The relationships between scientists and industry and between scientists and labor are a web of allegiances, professional responsibilities, career obligations, financial dependence, issues of ethics and integrity, personal prejudices and assumptions. Labor may mistrust intellectuals because of their dependence on industry funding and their perceived—or real—class alliances with management. Intellectuals may be equally mistrustful of labor, as seems to have been the case with Silverman. Management may be skeptical about the practical assistance academics can provide industry and wary of their tendency to put controversial judgments in print. Scientists become caught in a middle area, aware of the need to guarantee their financial and career survival by producing research, yet ethically bound to protect the public health.

Many of these themes can be found in the story of the Cotton Dust Project. The researchers ethically produced important research, yet often were circumspect in their conclusions and recommendations. Also, the researchers were not free from prejudice and assumption—from Drinker's assumption about the health of textile mill work to Silverman's derision of union members. Finally, the researchers remained aloof from the social, political, and human contexts in which they worked. When their research was completed, they moved on, leaving the textile work force little better off, if at all, than they were before.

Science, then, by itself is not an agent for social change, yet historical circumstances may make it so. If labor had been stronger among the textile mills in the South, if labor had been able to gain a political voice, if a popular crusade against byssinosis had existed, if researchers had made common cause with labor, if some in the textile industry had broken ranks, history might have been different.

As it was, cotton workers continued to labor in dusty conditions at great peril to their health for decades after the Harvard scientists published their work and moved on. It remained for others, much later, to move the issue of the health of textile workers into the political arena where the capacity to act and produce change is vested.

ENDNOTES

1. Phillip Drinker, *Atmospheric Conditions in the Cotton Textile Plants,* Special Bulletin No. 18 of the USDOL, Division of Labor Standards, June 1945.
2. Drinker had written a Division of Labor Standards Bulletin (#5) in 1941 entitled *Control of Welding Hazards in Defense Industries* for which Zimmer had provided an introduction.
3. Phillip Drinker and T. Hatch, *Industrial Dust,* McGraw-Hill, New York, 1936.
4. Mimi Conway, *Rise Gonna Rise: A Portrait of Southern Textile Workers,* Anchor Press/Doubleday, New York, 1979.
5. Saco-Lowell papers collection (SLP), Baker Library, Harvard Business School, Harvard University.
6. L. Silverman, *Air Contamination in Cotton Textile Processes,* National Safety Council News, April 1947.
7. *Textile Labor,* January 1946, p. 7.
8. On the Job, *Textile Labor,* July 19, 1947.
9. On the Job, *Textile Labor,* May 22, 1948.
10. F. G. Bishop to G. Perkel, 2/19/86.
11. It is not clear whether or not Silverman had honored this agreement in his first two published papers. He had *presented* them without approval, but as noted above Landau had made comments on Silverman's work at a date prior to their publication. Again, though, Silverman seems not to have been concerned with Landau's comments. So it's not quite clear what was going on at that time.
12. Present English Practice in Cotton Textile Process Ventilation, *Heating and Ventilation,* June 1949.
13. Mill Air Conditioning Made Easy, *Textile Labor,* October 2, 1948.
14. *Textile Labor,* November 20, 1948.
15. Heat Got 'Em, *Textile Labor,* April 2, 1949.
16. L. Silverman and F. Viles, The Determination of Cotton Textile Dusts in Air, *Textile Research Journal,* February 1950.
17. Silverman papers, Countway Library of Medicine, Harvard University.
18. B. H. Caminata et al., A Review of the Literature Relating to Afflictions of the Respiratory Tract in Individuals Exposed to Cotton Dust, *Public Health Bulletin No. 297,* p. 71, 1947.
19. L. Silverman and F. Viles, Progress Report on Ventilation for Cotton Textile Processes, *Heating and Ventilating Reference Section,* October 1947.
20. Determination of Starch and Cellulose with Anthrone, *Analytical Chemistry, 21,* 1949.
21. Silverman papers, Morgan to *Heating and Ventilation,* 7/16/47; Parker to Silverman, 5/7/47.

CHAPTER 6

"We Were Running from It, Really": Workers' Compensation and Byssinosis, 1950-1968

When six disabled cotton textile workers with byssinosis filed a lawsuit in 1979 in Alabama over their disease, one of the defendants they named was Liberty Mutual Insurance Company of Boston—the major carrier of workers' compensation insurance for the textile industry. The other defendants were some key executives of the firms, including a company physician, for whom they worked. The suit, *Williams v. Lanier et al.* [1], helped pry open the private doors of the textile industry, to give a view of the behind-the-scenes attitudes and actions of owners and their professional associates through the 1950s and 1960s where cotton dust was at issue.

The workers had sued the executives and insurer for failing to warn them about the hazards of cotton dust, providing them a false sense of security about the safety of their jobs, and failing to advise them about their medical condition after company-sponsored medical examinations. This case was unusual in that generally workers who are injured on the job cannot sue their employer, since doing so is barred by the exclusive remedy of workers' compensation. The peculiarities of Alabama law, however, allowed the suit to go forward.

In four years' time, the case was settled with all defendants except Liberty Mutual participating. A large sum of money changed hands, though the amount was not disclosed in keeping with terms of the settlement. Importantly, the process of discovery that was part of the lawsuit brought significant documents to light and required a number of employees of Liberty Mutual to be deposed by plaintiffs' attorneys. This information allows us to see some of the interrelationships among science, industry, and insurer and address certain key questions, among them: What in fact was a major insurer of the textile industry doing about cotton dust during the 1950s and 1960s? Was Liberty Mutual concerned about the issue? Did it warn its clients about the health hazards of cotton dust; did it urge its clients to reduce dust levels? Did potential liability for the payment of workers' compensation claims affect the behavior of the insurer? Was "science," research, going on concerning cotton dust during the 1950s and 1960s inside Liberty Mutual?

WORKERS' COMPENSATION AND
HEALTH AND SAFETY

When the no-fault workers' compensation systems first came into existence starting in 1911, advocates argued that these systems would provide benefits to hard-pressed injured workers, reduce the cost of litigation to all parties by moving such issues out of the courts, and provide financial incentives to industry to prevent accidents. "Experience rating"—charging higher insurance premiums to firms with poor safety records—was expected to foster accident prevention. In return for the expedited payment of benefits, workers would give up the right to sue their employers.

Although the workers' compensation system may have benefited many workers injured in industrial accidents, the political thrust for this widespread social insurance reform came from industry itself, seeking to limit liability and plan for and insure against future accident related expenses [2, 3].[1] Ironically, the insurance may actually have removed whatever pressures then existed on industry to prevent accidents by dampening the social outcry against the dreadful poverty that accompanied industrial injuries. Today, as workers' compensation costs remain a public issue, this social outcry—at least as presented by the media—has often been directed at the alleged attempts of "malingering" workers and their doctors and lawyers to bilk the system, rather than at the well-documented incidences of malfeasance of industry within the system [2, pp. 108-115].

Whatever the overall nature of the system, it is clear that workers' compensation has done little to prevent occupational disease or to compensate disease victims. Well into the 1980s, 90 percent of occupational lung disease claims were contested—although the system is supposed to be no-fault—and such cases frequently had to wait more than a year for settlement [4]. There is little evidence to indicate the system has greatly improved since that time [5, 6]. To fully explain this failure of the system would take us beyond the purposes of this current work, yet two points are worth mentioning. The first is that high financial stakes are at risk in claims for chronic disease, and so employers will naturally challenge such claims. Second, the nature of chronic occupational disease makes them relatively easy to challenge. Wooding and Levenstein explain:

> By and large the system is geared toward handling accidental injuries rather than occupational disease. . . . Thus, although workers' compensation is

---

[1] Discussions of workers' compensation and its origins are to be found in [2, 3].

supposed to be no-fault insurance, in the case of disease, employees must demonstrate the etiology of the illness. This requirement can be extremely difficult to meet when the illness is not recognizable as specific to a particular exposure or where the illness takes years to develop, as is frequently the case [2, p. 29].

The burden of proof, then, lies with the employee if the occupational origin of a disease is challenged [7-10].

The advent of workers' compensation also brought a new and wealthy actor to the occupational health scene—the insurers. Although some states barred private insurers and set up state funds as the sole carrier for workers' compensation, this was the exception rather than the rule. Private insurers dominated the system, and Boston-based Liberty Mutual became the major insurer for the textile industry.

Theoretically, under the "comp" system experience rating would encourage firms to work harder to prevent accidents, improve safety performance, and thereby lower their premium costs. It was expected that insurers would help industries to maintain safe premises. They would inspect plants for adequate safety practices, provide consulting services to firms that wanted to upgrade safety or simply learn about industrial hazards, and they would do safety research. These services would give insurers a strong role in occupational health activity. Liberty Mutual does provide such services, maintaining, for instance, a research and field services center in Hopkinton, Massachusetts.

This safety mission and the company's capacity to perform it placed Liberty Mutual in a position to know about byssinosis. Given that textile manufacturers only rarely had industrial hygiene staff, were reluctant to have close dealings with state agencies, and remained hostile to unions (textile unions also remained weak in the South in the 1950s and early 1960s), Liberty Mutual was the only party poised to act to alert companies and workers to the hazards of cotton dust.

What did Liberty Mutual know about cotton dust and when did it know it?

JOE M. BOSWORTH, MD

Perhaps one of the first persons inside Liberty Mutual to begin to take byssinosis seriously was Dr. Joe Bosworth who in 1950 became medical director of the company's Loss Prevention Department in its Atlanta-based Southern Division. He held the job for 15 years.

Bosworth had come to Atlanta from Florida in 1948 when, after his father's death, his disabled mother needed care. He had held a private practice in Florida and had been a flight surgeon in the Army Air Corps during World War II. In Atlanta, Liberty Mutual had hired him away from a job with the Veterans Administration to run Loss Prevention [11]. His new mission was to consult with policyholders to reduce compensable accidents and injuries. Bosworth's department also supplied information to underwriters to assist them in setting rates. When new business was sold, the department's engineers would sometimes visit the physical premises of a prospective client, review the conditions there, and then estimate anticipated costs. On occasion, Bosworth's staff would visit clients' plants to investigate changes in products or production processes, or an unusual loss experience [12]. Bosworth had engineers "assigned to each risk":

> They surveyed the risk, decided what might be needed . . . in the way of services from Liberty Mutual Insurance Company, and if they needed help, I was so appraised and an appointment was made and I would proceed to try to do what I could to help them; or a nurse may have gone with an engineer out of the same department, and if she wanted my help, I would go then [11, p. 9].

One of the factories Bosworth visited more often than most was Spring Mills, which had hired its own medical director and started an in-house occupational health program [11, p. 13]. Robert Amory, who had headed Nashua Manufacturing Company when it co-funded the Harvard Cotton Dust Project, was then a vice-president at Spring Mills. In the early 1950s, Spring Mills had become interested in byssinosis and there had been brief discussions between Amory and President Edwards of Saco-Lowell Shops about funding more cotton dust control studies, but Edwards eventually backed out [13, Edwards to Silverman, 11/2/50].[2]

Around 1952 or 1953, Bosworth himself became interested in investigating byssinosis problems, as in his visits to mills, including Spring Mills, he learned of reported complaints about respiratory problems and "Monday morning sickness." This interest and investigations continued into the 1960s. Bosworth reported his findings about health problems confidentially to mill management; he did not publish or make public any of his results. When questioned later about publication, he replied,

> I could have published rote [sic] information without the identification of a mill, but I was advised that that would not be the right thing to do. And I was not hungry for my name in print.
> Q. And who advised you that would not be the right thing to do?
> A. My boss.
> Q. Well, did he tell you why that would not be the right thing to do?
> R. Well, human beings have tendencies to develop hysteria when they get pieces of information, and some of which is incorrect, particularly when the medical profession don't [sic] know all of it, and I was called on several occasions to operations where hysteria broke out and it's pandemonium— not in the cotton mills—and I personally would thoroughly agree that it should not be done. As a matter of fact, when I called and asked, I said, "Do I need to?" And the answer was, "No" [11, pp. 83-84].

Bosworth's boss was W. H. Seymour, vice president in charge of Liberty Mutual's Loss Prevention in the company's Boston headquarters. So certainly at least one

---

[2] On Edwards' disinclination to continue such studies see [13].

top executive at Liberty Mutual—and no doubt others—was aware of a dangerous lung condition in the textile mills and decided to keep this information secret, apparently to prevent "hysteria."

Liberty Mutual's home office Loss Prevention was also aware of the work of the Harvard Cotton Dust Project. In 1954, R. G. McAllister of the New England Loss Prevention Department wrote to the Home Office about Silverman's progress report published in 1947 in the magazine *Heating and Ventilation.* McAllister quoted Silverman and Viles' recommendation that dust levels in opening and picking should be kept below 5 mgs per cubic meter "to eliminate complaints and nuisance problems." He further stated:

> To my way of thinking this represented an educated opinion on allowable limits to cotton dust in cotton textile processing mills and something we should have in our reference files. I consider it most unfortunate that we don't have copies of any of the results of research done in cotton textile plants by Dr. Silverman and Fred Viles. This is particularly unfortunate in as much as some of these were published in Heating and Ventilation Magazine which I think we have been taking over the years [14, McAllister to C. R. Williams and J. A. Houghton, 4/29/54].

In the *Williams v. Lanier et al.* case, Bosworth was deposed about the efforts of a disabled cotton mill worker to gain compensation. His answers offered a revealing insight into the attitudes of Liberty Mutual and its clients concerning byssinosis in the 1950s and early 1960s. He begins by saying,

> No, I think this was in the early Sixties when he got compensation. This one we found actually disabled, I think it was around '55 or—I have no notes on these or kept no notes, I was allowed to keep no notes—ah, it was all confidential at the time and, ah, the names as far as I'm concerned, are still confidential and I can't give them out.

When asked if he had ever determined the prevalence of byssinosis in the plants he visited, Bosworth replied:

> No. We didn't look for percentages. We were not looking for that. We were running from it, really.

When asked to explain, Bosworth answered:

> Well, we didn't want any more claims. The clients didn't want any more claims on 'em than we had to have.

He then added:

> And the industries, when they found out about it, of course, they were scared to death. They didn't know what was going to happen, because there could have been a wholesale cost to 'em, and they didn't want any part of it [11, pp. 87, 90].

Thus, byssinosis remained a curious kind of secret at Liberty Mutual and in the textile industry. Higher level officials at Liberty Mutual and managers in the industry were becoming increasingly aware of the problem, yet apparently "they didn't want any part of it." The 1950s seem a confusing period, where research on byssinosis was being done here and there, where knowledge—at least anecdotal—of byssinosis existed, where there was some knowledge of previous work on the disease, but all of this was not put together by Liberty Mutual, the only organization at the time that might have done so and had the responsibility to do so.

AN ENGLISHMAN'S VISIT

In 1954, Liberty Mutual representatives escorted an occupational physician from England, who was a Rockefeller Fellow, on a tour of cotton mills in Boston, the Carolinas, and Georgia. The doctor's name was Robert Murray, and he kept extensive notes of his observations (unlike Bosworth, he was allowed to keep them) [15, Robert Murray to R. Laufer, 9/20/84]. These notes provide an insightful view into the situation surrounding byssinosis at the time.

Murray assumed that some cotton mills had medical personnel, yet he met only one company physician during his tour and was puzzled because

> His function like that of other industrial medical officers appeared to have no relation to the effects of environment. . . . There did not appear to be any industrial hygienists employed in the industry and no figures were available of dust counts or bacterial counts.

He also recorded the Americans' denial of any serious respiratory diseases among the mill workers:

> The safety engineer of Liberty Mutual with whom I paid the visits in Spartanburg did not have any knowledge of cases of chest disease and the existence of anything resembling byssinosis was strenuously denied by most of the cotton spinners.

Yet Spartanburg was in the same region as Atlanta where Bosworth was already learning about respiratory problems in cotton mill workers. Moreover, Murray visited a small research center at one factory where he met a former stripper and grinder who gave "a typical history of byssinosis." This former card room worker said that "grinders cough" was well known among cotton mill workers and that anyone who worked in that part of the mill for more than two years was likely to be affected. Murray concluded that,

> . . . byssinosis or something akin to it does exist in the American cotton trade though not to the same extent as in Lancashire.

He then offered three possible reasons why the Americans were failing to investigate the problem:

1. In the South there is little or no trade union activity. This is frowned upon by the employers to such an extent that one mill whose work people wanted to form a union branch was closed for two years! The small numbers and wide scattering of mills does not encourage the gathering together of strippers and grinders to discuss their problems of health.

2. There is no compensation for chest disease in the cotton trade and consequently the insurance companies who have the facilities for investigation are not financially interested.

3. The problem is small in any case. This is very likely true. It may be that oiling has reduced the risk to negligible proportions or that the use of cotton pressed to standard or gin density and used within the crop year does not give rise to the development of the cause.

Summing up his cotton mill tour, Murray, with generous neutrality, wrote,

> I am very conscious of the fact that, at that time, byssinosis was not regarded as an occupational hazard in United States cotton mills. At that time, too, coal workers pneumoconiosis was not regarded as a hazard in the U.S. coal mines, nor was asbestos fully recognized. The reasons are not necessarily shameful. The priority at that time was given to silicosis...to the exclusion of other diseases.

Thus, in 1954 a visiting trained observer was easily able to pick up signs of byssinosis in U.S. cotton mills. But he was wrong on two counts: the problem was not small, and the insurance companies—namely, Liberty Mutual—were very financially interested. Liberty Mutual Insurance Company, with its "facilities for investigation," with its staff of industrial hygienists, engineers, physicians, and nurses, and as a major workers' compensation carrier for the U.S. textile industry, was avoiding treating seriously the problem of cotton dust related diseases.

By the mid-1950s, then, what did Liberty Mutual know or what should it have known? Bosworth's work was well under way by then and he was uncovering much evidence of respiratory problems among mill workers. Bosworth himself was often in contact with Amory and Spring Mills with its in-house occupational health program and continued interest in research on byssinosis. Within Bosworth's geographical area of responsibility, according to Murray, at least one factory was conducting research into byssinosis. Liberty Mutual was also aware of the Harvard Cotton Dust Project, and, despite McAllister's lament, could easily have found the full results of that work or spoken with the researchers themselves. Obviously, Liberty Mutual had an English connection and might have investigated the on-going work on byssinosis there. Even the work of Trice in North Carolina, who as early as 1939 had recommended cleaner cotton and adequate ventilation to relieve the respiratory problems of mill workers, was not obscure.

THE GEORGIA HEALTH DEPARTMENT CONNECTION

Dr. Lester M. Petrie served as the Director of the Industrial Hygiene Division of the Georgia Department of Public Health from 1941 to 1952. In 1952 the medical and engineering services of the division were separated, medical and nursing services going to a new Division of Occupational Health, chemical and engineering services remaining in the Division of Industrial Hygiene. Dr. Petrie was promoted to the position of the Director of the Preventable Diseases Branch of the Public Health Department, with supervisory responsibility for the two new divisions [16].

Bosworth later stated that Petrie was one of his earlier sources of information about byssinosis. The two were professional colleagues and apparently well acquainted; in May 1955 Petrie wrote a letter to Bosworth's boss, W. H. Seymour, commending Bosworth for his help on a particular project unrelated to byssinosis [16, Petrie to Seymour, 5/23/55].

One month earlier, Petrie had been alerted to possible byssinosis problems in the state. Dr. A. Worth Hobby, an Atlanta physician, wrote him the following:

> May I thank you for the information on Public Health Bulletin #297 on Cotton Dust Exposure. . . . I have gone over the material available and believe that we have a case of byssinosis, but I am unable to prove that it *is* such a case. It lacks one of the criteria which is: a recovery as soon as removed from the dust area. This patient got worse after leaving the dust area and has progressed since that time instead of returning to normal. Therefore, I presume it is not a case of byssinosis [16, Hobby to Petrie, 4/8/55].

Hobby's patient may well have been suffering Grade III byssinosis—irreversible and progressive—according to a scale for the disease later developed by Richard Schilling. As far as we have been able to determine, the doctor's letter provoked no investigation.

By the evidence available, not until 1958 did additional byssinosis-related activity occur in the Georgia Public Health Department. In February of that year, Bosworth brought to Petrie two samples of cotton for analysis in the state laboratory. The samples had come from mills located near each other and owned by the same company. In one of the plants, the mill nurse had reported that workers had been experiencing byssinotic symptoms for about six months. The affected employees all worked in the card room. Employees in the second mill seemed not to be having any problems, as far as was reported. Petrie, on behalf of Liberty Mutual's Bosworth, asked the head of the state laboratory to determine if the cotton was biologically contaminated [16, Petrie to Sunkes, 2/12/58].

While the state laboratory was analyzing the cotton samples, Petrie consulted with Dr. Paul Joliet of the U.S. Public Health Service Regional Office in Atlanta. Apparently, Joliet had never heard of any suspected byssinosis cases in the United States, and was interested. Joliet offered to lend a medical epidemiologist to the State Public Health Department if it was possible to gain access to the textile plant where problems had been reported. Joliet, in turn, contacted Dr. Harold Magnuson, chief of the USPHS Occupational Health Program, who agreed the lead was worth pursuing [16, Joliet to Magnuson, 5/6/58]. Petrie called Bosworth to find out if Liberty Mutual would release the name of the company, but he was out of town and unavailable [16, Petrie to Joliet, 5/6/58].

In a few days, the state lab reported back that both samples of cotton were in fact biologically contaminated. At about the same time, Bosworth responded to Petrie's request who passed on the reply to Joliet. Joliet wrote:

> I am sorry to advise you that Dr. Joe Bosworth, Liberty Mutual Insurance Company, is not at liberty to divulge the names of the industrial plants. Although he would presumably like to see the investigation pursued further with our help, the industrial management has asked him to consider the information confidential and privileged. Both Dr. Bosworth and I agree that the evidence we have at present is insufficient to justify making an issue. We will both keep our eyes and ears open and if further suspected outbreaks come to our attention will reopen the investigation [16, Petrie to Joliet, 5/11/58].

The work on byssinosis did continue in Georgia after this point, the subject of our next two chapters, but without the help of Liberty Mutual Insurance Company or Dr. Joe Bosworth. When Richard Schilling, the British investigator of byssinosis, was invited to Georgia in 1960, Petrie again asked Bosworth for help, this time to gain Schilling entrance to cotton mills. Bosworth was not able to help him [11]. And so it went.

THE 1960s

By the 1960s it seems clear that Liberty Mutual was well aware of byssinosis. Two additional pieces of evidence lend credence to this, and especially of their knowledge of the work in Britain.

In 1960, George Huckeba, a Liberty Mutual staff industrial hygienist, did an engineering study of a Southern cotton textile plant. He recommended improvement of ventilation in the card room based on the British-suggested total dust standard of 1 mg per cubic meter [14, Huckeba document, and Van Houten deposition].

In March 1964, Charles Cole, an industrial hygienist working out of Liberty Mutual's Atlanta office, met a U.S. Public Health Service industrial hygienist, Elbridge Morrill, Jr., at a course in industrial ventilation held in North Carolina. Cole asked Morrill for information on threshold limit values and methods of sampling for cotton dust, but he said he did not need specific information on byssinosis. Morrill sent him a long letter reviewing recent articles on cotton dust and also a bibliography on byssinosis. Morrill commented that the American Conference of Governmental Industrial Hygienists (ACGIH) was going to act at the end of April 1964 on a committee recommendation that a threshold limit value (TLV) be set at 1 mg per cubic meter for cotton dust [14, Morrill to Cole, 4/2/64].

WAS LIBERTY MUTUAL DOING SCIENTIFIC RESEARCH?

Not until the 1970s did *any* element of the textile industry admit that byssinosis was a serious problem in the United States. Liberty Mutual claimed at the time of *Williams v. Lanier et al.* that it did not begin industrial hygiene evaluations of the cotton dust problem until the late 1960s. The Industrial Hygiene Field Services of Liberty Mutual provides consulting services to policy-holders similar to that of the Loss Prevention Departments. The then head of Industrial Hygiene Field Services, Russell Van Houten, stated,

> . . . [W]e were not working on the basis that cotton dust was a problem in American mills until after 1967. . . . We began to review sampling methods in 1968 and began sampling in 1969 [12].

This may very well be true. It is difficult to determine exactly Liberty Mutual's internal research efforts on the problems inside textile mills; it is not public information and so we must rely on inference and on the occasional glimpses inside an insurance firm afforded by such cases as *Williams v Lanier et al.* Nevertheless, we do know that Liberty Mutual was very careful to narrowly define what it deemed scientific research.

From the 1960s into the 1980s, Allen Cudworth was Director of Research for Liberty Mutual. As a vice-president of the company he supervised both its Industrial Hygiene Field Service, and so was Van Houten's superior, and its Research Center at Hopkinton. When quizzed about the firm's research operations, Cudworth testified that the findings of the Hopkinton research facility, which tended to focus mainly on noise-related research, were published in refereed scientific journals. He explained that, "In general, research projects are not done for a specific policy-holder, and therefore almost all research data is published" [17, p. 25]. He went on to state that research done for particular clients generally was not published [17, p. 27].

Cudworth also emphasized that industrial hygienists—the personnel who would be most likely to work on a cotton dust problem in a textile mill—working out of Hopkinton "do not do research" [17, p. 40]. Rather, they do "surveys" aimed at "evaluating the level of cotton dust" [17, p. 45].

He had carefully chosen his words. Cudworth's answer echoed the distinctions with which Bosworth had answered a question about whether or not he did research when he worked for the company:

> Not according to my definition of the word. My definition of the word says that you discreetly and in depth study and relieve all possibilities. Our study was not really research; it was merely trying to find out, if we could, what

were the predominant causes of the symptoms that were available, that were present [11].

However the company's representatives phrased it, plainly, scientific activity was going on—and on-going—at Liberty Mutual. Perhaps its science was not of an extremely high quality, but frequently case reports are published in medical journals to alert the medical community to a health problem or to see whether or not they will bring forward other clinicians or researchers who have similar or other useful experiences that might contribute to explaining an issue. Furthermore, if the insurer had regularly published reports about respiratory problems in the mills, the industry could not have steadfastly maintained, as it did for so long, that there was no byssinosis problem in the United States. This reporting might have given government investigators the basis for insisting that industry cooperate with public health inspectors and provide them access to mills, which was denied for so long. But Liberty Mutual did not publish such case reports.

CONCLUSION

In his controversial and seminal book *Death on the Job,* Daniel Berman has suggested, as we have discussed in Chapter 1, that a hegemonic social structure with a common approach to workers' health and safety has dominated the field since early in the 20th century. Berman calls the practitioners of this approach the "compensation-safety apparatus," comprised of insurance companies and their associations, key professional organizations, business-funded research founda-tions, and standard setting institutes. He writes that

> . . . they believe in voluntary action by the private sector rather than govern-
> ment regulation of working conditions; they support common ventures
> and do not criticize each other publicly . . . and they claim to be disinter-
> ested and scientifically neutral between management and labor. All of
> them . . . share industry's concern with keeping its cost to a minimum
> [9, pp. 75-76].

The notion of a "compensation-safety" apparatus helps us understand the behavior of Liberty Mutual and its employees and representatives. It was not that Liberty Mutual did not care about byssinosis, it cared very much indeed. Nor was it the case that they were conducting no research on byssinosis in the 1950s or that industrial physicians like Bosworth were not concerned about the problem. Yet, the combined social and economic links among occupational health professionals, their employers, and the insurance industry created a shared hegemonic view of workers' health and safety that allowed them to keep the knowledge of byssinosis to themselves.

What is reasonable to expect of physicians, industrial hygienists, and engineers who are the employees of insurance companies or of industry? In this context, a serious problem emerges between a professional ethic or public health responsibility on the one hand and the economic bonds and responsibilities of employment on the other. Without a counter-hegemonic force, as emerged with the strong worker and consumer health movements of the 1960s, or of a more or less serendipitous constellation of social forces, as existed during the banning of the suck shuttle, economic bonds may too often outweigh professional responsibility. Such are the lessons to be learned from the story of Liberty Mutual Insurance Company and byssinosis.

POSTSCRIPT

As Elbridge Morrill had predicted to Liberty Mutual's industrial hygienist, the ACGIH did make a recommendation on cotton dust in the Spring of 1964. Without any new American research findings, its Threshold Limits Committee backed a TLV for cotton dust of 1 mg per cubic meter. Members of the committee included representatives of the U.S. Public Health Service and other federal agencies, state departments of health and labor, universities as well as private industry. Its conclusion: work in cotton mills was "safe with medical supervision of workers" at the recommended TLV [18].

The ACGIH was founded in 1938, an offshoot of the American Industrial Hygiene Association. Relatively free from corporate control, in comparison to private professional groups concerned with health and safety standards such as the American Society of Safety Engineers and the Council on Occupational Health, one of its major functions was to develop exposure limits for industry and government. Indeed, when OSHA was established in 1971, it adopted wholesale many of ACGIH's recommendations. But as the ACGIH exposure limits themselves were merely recommended, few if any industries adopted them.

In setting its standard on cotton dust, ACGIH had adopted a new procedure, widely distributing 10,000 copies of a "Notice of Intent." The purpose of this notice was to inform industry about planned changes and additions to the list of recommendations for controlling toxic exposures. Thus, the committee's recommendation undoubtedly reached both the textile industry and its insurers. For two years after 1964, the organization solicited comments on its recommendation, and in 1966 the measure became the official ACGIH standard, and the new standard was announced widely [19].

Through the whole course of action, the ACGIH recommendation was remarkably non-controversial, perhaps because it was of little practical consequence. Although tantamount to being the first recognition by a major professional organization in this country that byssinosis might be a problem in the United States, the recommendation incited little change in industrial practices. ACGIH recommendations were just that: advisory, unenforceable, and in this case not controversial. The standard made little if any difference.

ENDNOTES

1. Much of this chapter is based on papers uncovered through this lawsuit. One of the authors of this current work, Charles Levenstein, served as an expert witness for the plaintiffs and was given copies of documents and depositions in the case. Notes will state "Lawsuit" to indicate this source.

2. C. Levenstein and J. Wooding, *The Point of Production*, Guilford Press, New York, 1999.

3. P. S. Barth and H. A. Hunt, *Workers' Compensation and Work-Related Illness and Disease,* Chapter 2, MIT Press, Cambridge, Massachusetts, 1980.

4. Policy Statement: "Workers' Compensation and the Prevention of Occupational Disease," *American Journal of Public Health,* Feb. 1984. See also *Workers' Compensation and Work-Related Illness and Disease* [3].

5. M. Silverstein, Remembering the Past, Acting on the Future, *New Solutions, 5*:4, p. 80, 1995.

6. L. I. Boden, Workers' Compensation in the United States: High Costs, Low Benefits, *American Review of Public Health, 16,* pp. 180-218, 1995.

7. There were two exceptions to the general rule on disease claims: asbestosis and silicosis, both of which were strongly linked to tuberculosis and could be identified fairly straightforwardly with radiography. Silicosis became a national *cause celebre* after 700 people died and another 1500 were disabled in the 1930s Gauley Bridge disaster in West Virginia. Thousands of workers on the Union Carbide tunnel construction project there had been exposed to hazardous silica dust and, to curb employers' potential liability, workers' compensation was extended to survivors of the disaster. For a complete study of silicosis see [8-10].

8. D. Rosner and G. Markowitz, *Deadly Dust: Silicosis and the Politics of Occupational Disease in Twentieth-Century America,* Princeton University Press, Princeton, 1991.

9. Daniel Berman, *Death on the Job: Occupational Health and Safety Struggles in the United States,* Monthly Review Press, New York, 1978.

10. D. Ozonoff, *Workers' Compensation for Silicosis,* paper presented at the American Association for the Advancement of Science, Detroit, May 1983.

11. Bosworth deposition. Lawsuit.

12. Van Houten deposition. Lawsuit.

13. Saco-Lowell papers collection (SLP), Baker Library, Harvard Business School, Harvard University.

14. Liberty Mutual papers. Lawsuit.

15. Correspondence from Robert Murray to R. Laufer of the Southern Poverty Law Center, 9/20/84.

16. Papers of the Director, Georgia Department of Public Health, Georgia Archives.

17. Cudworth deposition, Lawsuit.

18. ACGIH, "1965 Documentation of Threshold Limit Values."

19. On the procedures of the Threshold Limits Committee, particularly regarding the cotton dust recommendation, see the report by the Committee's chairman, Herbert E. Stokinger, "Modus Operandi of Threshold Limits Committee of ACGIH," *Transactions of the 26th Annual Meeting of the ACGIH,* Philadelphia, Pennsylvania, pp. 23-29, April 25-28, 1964.

CHAPTER 7

Georgia and the "Mysterious Disease" of Byssinosis

Almost from the start of his planned research project on byssinosis, Dr. Harry E. Dickson was placed on the defensive by Georgia's manufacturers [1].

Dickson had succeeded Dr. Lester Petrie as head of Georgia's Division of Occupational Health and almost immediately took up the cotton dust issue. In November 1959 he sent a memorandum to the state's local and regional health departments seeking their support and cooperation on a study called "Health Evaluation of the Textile Worker in Georgia."

About 100,000 Georgians then worked in 175 textile plants in the state, making it the third largest producer of cotton textiles in the country. Dickson, an occupational physician, had become aware of the respiratory problems in the work force while serving as Petrie's research assistant, and he continued to believe the problem was too important to be ignored. He had been born and educated in Tennessee, interned in Memphis, and taught in Mississippi. He had worked for private industry, as a physician for Union Carbide Nuclear Company in Oak Ridge, and had just completed a master's degree in public health from Harvard. Dickson had at his disposal a team of researchers interested in byssinosis who had originally come together under Petrie to study the kaolin industry in Georgia [2].

In making his case to the smaller health departments, Dickson told them it was no surprise that byssinosis had been overlooked even though it was a disease that had been known for 200 years. Its diagnosis, he said, depended on a doctor taking a patient's occupational history and few physicians had the time to do that. In addition,

> The few small studies in the textile workers of the United States have revealed negative or inconclusive results; however, no large scale survey had been made with a thorough evaluation of the respiratory system.

Dickson was proposing to adapt the techniques developed in the kaolin study for use in studying the textile industry. This meant a "thorough clinical evaluation" of the workers, especially of all cardio-respiratory factors, including chest X-rays. Each subject's work environment would be evaluated and dust, temperature, and humidity would be assessed. Finally, Dickson noted, "bacterial, chemical, and pharmacological studies are projected." He gave no indication of how many workers would be involved.

He was careful, however, to set certain parameters for the reporting of results. Findings would go to workers, their physicians, and company doctors. The firms involved would receive a summary of the study information, but it would not identify individual employees and it would not be distributed until the end of the project. In addition, Dickson wrote, "No scientific data will be published without the approval of the participating industries and only then without identifying individual patients." Finally, local medical society approval of the project would also be required [2, Dickson memo to Local and Regional Health Departments, 11/4/59].

Reaction was not long in coming. When Dr. G. B. Creagh, Director of Georgia's Public Health District #31, received Dickson's letter, he brought it to the attention of a group of textile company officials. They formulated a set of questions designed to protect owners' interests, which Creagh then passed back to Dickson:

1. Is this study going to turn up compensable cases under the Workman's Compensation laws?
2. Will information come out of this study that will result in recommendations involving structural changes for correction of the mills?
3. Is this study being discussed with the Georgia Textile Manufacturers Association? [2, Creagh to Dickson, 11/16/59].

At the end of December, Public Health Department officials, including Dickson and Dr. John Venable, met with Ted M. Forbes, executive vice-president and top staff person of the Georgia Textile Manufacturers Association (GTMA). Forbes became the point man in the effort to block Dickson's byssinosis study. He reported on his meeting with Public Health Department officials in a long letter to Morris Bryan, Jr., head of Jefferson Mills; Jefferson Mills had apparently asked for Public Health Department assistance in establishing an occupational health program. Copies of the letter were sent to all GTMA officers.

According to Forbes, Dickson first described the proposed study, pointing out that it was not the Department's objective to search for workers' compensation cases, but that it might be possible to determine a "safe" limit for cotton dust concentrations. Dickson emphasized that the Department would make no recommendations without a comprehensive understanding of the conditions in the mills that might require such a standard. He added that the plan was to study 1000 workers.

Forbes' rebuttal was strong and uncompromising, and presents a litany of themes, concerns, and strategies that were to recur often in the later history of industry-researcher relations. He explained his objections to the study in this way:

1. Since there is absolutely no evidence that any pulmonary diseases exist among Georgia textile mill workers, by reason of their employment environment, and since the performance records, in terms of both productive work and job attendance have never indicated any evidence of the existence of any pulmonary disease that would affect their health or the performance of their duties, it seems to us that funds might be expended for some more useful purpose to study health conditions that are known to exist.

2. . . . [W]hen there is a public announcement about the allocation of funds for this project, or the beginnings of the study itself, our industry will be automatically indicted in the minds of the general public. . . .

3. The knowledge that such a study is being made . . . will add to such difficulties as presently exist in procuring sufficient manpower to operate our industry.

4. . . . [A] high percentage of textile mill employees will soon imagine that they have the symptoms . . . , and people who never heard of the disease will soon be convinced that they have it, and that sort of mass hysteria can do a great deal of damage.

5. . . . [T]he very fact that the survey is being made and that this matter is having the attention of the Health Department is all that will be needed to encourage the damage suit lawyers to initiate and urge the passage of amendments to our Workmen's Compensation Act, which will provide compensation for alleged occupational disease in our industry [2, Forbes to Bryan, 12/29/59].

Dr. Venable had tried to reassure Forbes that the results of the study were likely to be negative, but Forbes insisted that the public relations problems would come no matter what the results were. Venable further argued that no findings would be published without industry's consent. Finally, he urged Forbes to go with Dickson to meet the kaolin employers who he said could assure Forbes that the Health Department was capable of effectively dealing with delicate issues. Forbes remained unconvinced.

In his letter, Forbes reported to the owners that he had received no assurance that officials would halt the investigation if they received funding for it. He suggested further meetings between owners and the Health Department officials. He believed he had created some doubt in the researchers' minds about,

> the wisdom of making the survey, as to its need, and as to the reaction that will result in the minds of Georgia textile mill employers, so they may take another look at it [2, Forbes to Bryan, 12/29/59].

Dickson, however, remained quite insistent that more research had to be done on cotton dust. This he made clear in a letter to Forbes dated January 18, 1960. Dickson once again reminded Forbes that any study would be conducted discreetly, and once more urged Forbes to talk with kaolin industry employers, pledging to go with him. The main point of Dickson's letter was to invite Forbes to a meeting with the co-investigators on the research. They were, on the medical side, Dr. Ross McLean of Emory University in Atlanta and, for engineering, Dr. Clyde Orr of Georgia Institute of Technology [2, Dickson to Forbes, 1/18/60].

Forbes immediately responded, reiterating his concerns:

> As I assured you all at our previous conferences, if there had ever been any sign of the existence of this mysterious disease among Georgia textile mill employees it would have come to light somewhere and at sometime during the 33 years with which I have been associated with this industry.

He requested Dickson delay the meeting with McLean and Orr until the end of the state legislative session because he was involved with matters pending there. Then, he again stated his worries about the image of the industry:

> I hope that you . . . will appreciate the sincerity of our position in this matter, and understand that while we have no fear of your revealing any general impairment of the health of any substantial number of textile mill employees as a result of the environment in which they work causing them to be afflicted with the mysterious disease of byssinosis, they do fear greatly, and I think rightly so, the inevitable effects that such a survey would have on the public relations and the industrial relations of our industry [2, Forbes to Dickson, 1/20/60].

Forbes' meeting with McLean and Orr put on hold, McLean and others went forward with their plans. They submitted a well-conceived and well-written proposal to the U.S. Public Health Service (although in later years Dr. McLean came to think of it as overly ambitious) and a review committee from the U.S. Department of Health, Education, and Welfare met about the research in March. The issue of industry cooperation seemed to present a serious stumbling block, and in a letter to Forbes about the review committee meeting, Dickson indicated as much:

> After much study about this matter, it is felt that a study is indicated . . . and we feel that a pilot study could be carried out without doing irreparable harm to the textile industry . . . However, in order to carry out a program of this type, we must have the full understanding and cooperation of the participating industries and we would in no way desire to handicap the good relations that the Georgia Department of Public Health has had in the past with the Georgia textile industries [2, Dickson to Forbes, 3/29/60].[1]

Petrie, who was to be a consultant on the research project, also wrote to Forbes. His tone seems both exasperated and angry:

> The Georgia Department of Health did not create this problem. It is your problem. Over the years, we have received many, many complaints. We have

---

[1] Interview with Dr. Ross McLean conducted on 6/16/83 by Charles Levenstein.

not done too much about it because too many of the complaints have been anonymous, and because of their anonymity, we have discounted them. I am sending you a thermofax copy of the most recent complaint.

He added that Emory University's Department of Medicine had received requests from physicians all over the state for information on the respiratory health of textile workers. He concluded by bluntly offering Forbes this challenge:

Can the Georgia Textile Manufacturers Association Inc. go on record stating that without question, cotton dust has no effect on the respiratory system of textile workers? If so, can such medical evidence be furnished? Do you have a medical advisory committee which can supply this information? [2, Petrie to Forbes, 3/30/60].

On April 13, 1960 the delayed meeting between the researchers and manufacturers took place at Grady Hospital in Atlanta. In addition to Forbes and O. B. Moore from the GTMA, textile companies represented were Bibb Manufacturing, Riegel Textile, Graniteville Company, Swift Manufacturing, and West Point Manufacturing. Dr. Paul Austin, the Medical director of West Point Manufacturing, was the only industry physician present. Forbes wrote a detailed report on the conference, the substance of which was confirmed in an interview with Dr. McLean [3].

McLean opened the meeting with a personal story. He told of being questioned by three Georgia physicians at a conference on internal medicine about pulmonary disease in cotton textile workers. He was unable to answer their questions. Subsequently, he had investigated the questions and had become convinced that there was a definite relationship between cotton dust exposure and mill worker respiratory problems.

Dickson then outlined the planned research and Forbes outlined industry concerns as he had previously stated them to Dickson. McLean responded by reviewing in some detail what was known about byssinosis and presenting a letter from two British researchers, who were expected to visit the United States soon.

Dr. Austin, the industrial physician from West Point Manufacturing, then made some comments that revealed he already had fairly extensive knowledge of byssinosis. According to Forbes, Austin pointed out

... that some of the symptoms that have been found might result from such things as insecticides . . . , defoliating chemicals . . . and the large amount of dust resulting from the harvesting of cotton by mechanical pickers. He observed that some studies that have been made by the West Point Manufacturing Company show that low grade cotton gives the most trouble.

When the U.S. Public Health Service had done chest x-rays of West Point workers in 1946, according to Austin, it had reported a very low incidence of pulmonary disease, including tuberculosis. Chest x-rays, he agreed though, "are not a positive diagnosis of byssinosis, and that to a large extent the doctors must depend upon what people tell them about the trouble they have." He added that the problem may lie in the "sensitivity of certain individuals to certain types of dust and lint" [3].

The meeting went on, with Forbes pushing to get more details on the proposed study and McLean, Petrie, and Dickson pushing to get industry support. At one point Dr. Orr of Georgia Tech declared, again according to Forbes, "that he was interested only in studying samples of air and is not concerned at all with the health aspects of this problem." In the end, Forbes insisted that GTMA had neither the right nor the authority to recommend cooperation to its membership. The association would remain "neutral." If any member inquired about the study, Forbes would provide only the facts that came out of the meeting [3].

The day after the meeting, Dickson wrote to the U.S. Public Health Service explaining GTMA's neutral stance. He optimistically added that the Health Department

> has had excellent relations for many years with our textile industries. Our meeting of April 13 has helped to maintain this relationship. The sponsoring institutions as well as the textile industries have improved mutual understanding of our joint needs and responsibilities. It is certain that the meeting did not close the door to the study [4, Dickson to Syme, 4/14/60].

Forbes communicated with his constituents; with his letter to the association's membership he attached a copy of the research proposal. He outlined the association's objections to the study and commented about the April 13 meeting:

> We were positively assured by the sponsors that our apprehensions about the public and industrial relations implications and about the potential effects upon our workmen's compensation law and its costs were "completely ungrounded." Needless to say, we did not admit the validity of that conclusion [5].

Forbes reiterated the official neutral stance: the association would not recommend cooperation and participation, nor would it urge that its members not participate. "The decision," he wrote, "is one to be made solely by the authorized officials of [a] particular company." He explained that the wording of GTMA's statement had been communicated to the National Institutes of Health which was deciding whether to fund the project, and if the federal money came through the research study would probably go forward [6].

But the federal money did not come through, as the National Institutes of Health declined to fund the research study; without doubt this must have been a major disappointment for Dickson and his team. In later years, trying to account for the failure of funding, Dr. McLean believed that the plan had been too ambitious and that lack of cooperation from the manufacturers had probably helped doom the project [McLean interview].

Forbes may have won the battle but remained concerned about the war: he continued to worry about the scientists' growing interest in the issue. He feared the byssinosis problem was gaining such momentum, both at the Health Department and among academics in the state, that inevitably a study would be done. He wrote the head of GTMA:

> While I think we need to be very careful about indicating any major interest in this question of byssinosis, I am not at all sure that our friends over at the State Health Department and at Emory University are going to let us ignore it completely [2, Forbes to McKenney, 7/12/60].

Forbes' concern was such that almost any action by the Health Department became cause for alarm. When he heard at a meeting of the state Water Quality Council that the Health Department was developing an interest in air pollution, focusing mainly on radiation problems, his reaction was the following:

> I am quite sure that once they get into it they will involve all major industries in our state, including ours, as well as the paper and rayon industries who are always worried about the odors that emanate from their plants [2, Forbes to McKenney, 7/12/60].

He had reason to worry. Dickson was already planning a series of articles on occupational health in Georgia aimed at "making the average practitioner in Georgia more cognizant of the various occupational diseases" [4, Dickson to Petrie and McLean, 3/17/60], and the first of these was to be on pulmonary disease and cotton textile work [7]. His fears only mounted that summer when two key investigators of byssinosis in Britain visited Georgia and held a seminar at the same hospital where Forbes and the manufacturers had met with Dickson and his research team.

SCHILLING AND McKERROW IN GEORGIA

When R. S. F. Schilling and Colin McKerrow arrived in Atlanta that July, Forbes was invited to the party, actually a luncheon and seminar. Forbes could not attend, but Frank Carter, secretary of the owners' association, took his place.

Carter returned from the seminar with the British researchers armed with a wealth of information which he summarized in a three-page memorandum for Forbes. In Britain, Carter told Forbes, both deaths and disability pensions due to byssinosis had increased dramatically since 1942, right after the disease had been recognized and made compensable. Schilling and McKerrow had recently surveyed 722 cotton mill workers in England.

> The survey was made through the cooperation of the union, "since all mills are organized," of the company management, and of the employees themselves. Some opposition was encountered, for industrial executives "could not believe" that there was dust enough to cause any trouble. This was disproved, according to the doctors, in the very mills that complained.

It was the mills that used low-grade cotton and made coarse goods that had more trouble than those using higher grades of cotton and making finer products.

Some substance in the cotton, still unidentified, was causing the disease, Schilling and McKerrow had said. Carter found it significant that the researchers focused their attention exclusively on the card room. He wrote:

> Both doctors . . . referred only to the card rooms of the mills, for this room seems to be the one in which there is the most "dust" and the most byssinosis patients. It was determined that "dust" is emitted from three different places on the card machine and that the presence of byssinosis in employees working "right at" the cards was high; it was low in persons working "near" the cards; and it was remote in persons working "at a distance" from the card machines. No other room in a cotton mill was mentioned during the entire discussion.

Carter concluded with his analysis of how the Georgia textile industry had been damaged by the seminar:

> 1. One or two of the Georgia Department of Health officials took copious notes, and I imagine the Department will press harder than ever the plan to make a survey of the Georgia mills, to see to what extent byssinosis exists among the textile workers. This plan was not mentioned, however; and
> 2. The young doctors who were present seemed fascinated by the discussion of something which, admittedly, U.S. doctors know little about, and there is the possibility that they will start "looking for" byssinosis now whenever they come across bronchial troubles in their practice [2, Carter to Forbes, 7/12/60].

The President of GTMA, Paul L. McKenney, Jr., shared Forbes' alarm at what was happening. He suggested that Forbes circulate information on byssinosis and a shortened version of Carter's meeting notes among the membership and then to talk to their medical personnel. He believed that ". . . the matter is already of such interest to the Georgia Department of Public Health that we would be expecting too much to think that they are going to drop it immediately." Privately, he hoped the rumor about an air pollution study was true as he thought it might take the spotlight off the cotton textile industry and byssinosis:

> Should they go into a survey of "air pollution." My guess would be that that would get a lot more publicity than the other survey [2, McKenney to Forbes, 7/14/60].

Forbes was less sanguine in his views, and he remained tenacious in his concern about cotton dust disease:

> Whether we like it or not, I am afraid that this is another example of governmental interference which will be difficult to stop. I did everything that I possibly could through the state Department of Health when the matter first came up months ago, and I was unable to convince any of them...that the existence of the disease or the hazard is insufficient to warrant any sort of study or survey. Therefore, I think we need to warn our members that they may be confronted with such a study so that they will be prepared for it [2, Forbes to McKenney, 7/18/60].

Accordingly, Forbes sent out an alert and urged the manufacturers to give "careful attention to plant conditions which may cause this problem to assume increasing importance." With the alert he sent a version of Carter's notes edited so as to prevent any problems from developing if it fell into "the wrong hands." He also mentioned the rumor about an air pollution study and suggested, although this was not in Carter's memorandum, that Georgia Department of Public Health officials had taken copious notes at the Schilling and McKerrow seminar in order to incorporate a study of byssinosis prevalence into the air pollution investigation [8].

Meanwhile, in December 1960, Dickson's article, co-authored by McLean, "Pulmonary Disease and Cotton Processing," was published in the *Journal of the Medical Association of Georgia*. The piece contained an excellent review of the literature on byssinosis and included a clearly stated estimate of the potential extent of the problem in Georgia. The authors concluded there was an urgent need for epidemiological study of the disease in the United States.

In March of 1961, a resident in occupational medicine at the University of Michigan, Dr. E. A. Shaptini, published another review of the byssinosis literature. Shaptini's review was comprehensive, but sent a mixed message to the U.S. textile industry. On the one hand, as he wrote,

> Though only a small percentage of workers in the cotton textile industry is exposed to a serious dust hazard, because of the great number of workers in the industry the extent of the problem becomes worthy of consideration [9, p. 95].

On the other hand, however:

> In a general way, it has been noted that the incidence is greater in England and Russia, and less (almost none) in the United States. Several reasons are suggested for this difference, such as the more rapid turnover of personnel in the United States mills, thereby not having workers exposed for a sufficient number of years; better ventilation in the U.S. mills, etc. [9, p. 97].

In May, GTMA sent both the Dickson and McLean and the Shaptini articles to its membership. Forbes wrote that he was not endorsing the notion that byssinosis was a serious problem, but because of increasing government interest in the issue he wanted to keep the membership informed:

> . . . a careful reading of these articles should give our industry some encouragement because in spite of the amount of study and research that has been devoted to this subject, there has been produced very little evidence that this pulmonary disease is prevalent in the cotton manufacturing industry or that it exists at all to any appreciable extent.

But Forbes had another reason for his vigilance. One of the members of the association was involved in a workers' compensation case involving a card room employee who claimed he had silicosis.

We are told that during the discussions, legal and medical, about this case, the word "byssinosis" has been mentioned.

Finally, Forbes alerted GTMA members to the Georgia Department of Public Health survey of industrial air pollution, which by May was no longer a rumor but a reality [10].

THE AIR POLLUTION STUDY
AND THE GTMA

GTMA had received in March "numerous" phone calls and letters from members about a Georgia Department of Health mail questionnaire on air pollution. Forbes wrote to Dr. Venable, who had become Department of Public Health Director, to complain about the failure of the Department to consult with industry representatives.

> Rightfully, I think members of our Association are raising a question with respect to the necessity for a study of this kind, and particularly the propriety of being asked to furnish certain production and manufacturing data which they would regard as being strictly confidential [4, Forbes to Venable, 3/29/61].

Venable quickly apologized. Consultations had taken place with Associated Industries of Georgia, the state Chamber of Commerce, several industries, he told Forbes, but the questionnaires had inadvertently gone out to textile owners before a conference had been arranged with GTMA. Venable was conciliatory and said he was sure the textile firms' concerns could be worked out [4, Venable to Forbes, 4/4/61].

While they studied community air quality control over the next year, Public Health officials, as Forbes had indeed predicted, tenaciously kept watch for opportunities to investigate byssinosis. Such an opportunity came in the summer of 1962 when several companies in Bartow, Floyd, and Polk counties began discussion with the local Tuberculosis Association about chest x-rays for their mill workers. Agnes Quarles, secretary of the TB Association, contacted Dr. Petrie, and he suggested a more extensive survey of chronic pulmonary disease in two of the counties. When the firms indicated an interest, Petrie suggested the Association call in Dr. Walter Dunbar, Chairman of the Respiratory Disease Sub-committee of the Georgia Tuberculosis Association, and Dr. McLean. Petrie also forwarded correspondence for Forbes on byssinosis, and then sent a copy of his letter to Forbes [4, Petrie to Quarles, 8/22/62].

Petrie's letter, not surprisingly, galvanized Forbes who immediately wrote to all GTMA members in the three counties:

> I do not know who made the request for chest X-ray surveys of textile mill employees . . . but I would judge from Dr. Petrie's letter that the request

may be used as an excuse for continuing the efforts to study the prevalence of byssinosis . . . frankly, we have tried to discourage surveys dealing with this problem [2, Forbes to GTMA members in Bartow, Floyd, and Polk counties, 8/23/62].

The next day Forbes wrote to the whole membership about industrial air pollution and warned that health officials were still looking for evidence of byssinosis. He also told them to pay attention to what was happening in the state legislature where the Health Department had proposed bills to regulate air quality and occupational health. "This problem," he noted, should receive "very serious consideration and attention" [11].

One can only imagine how Forbes greeted the news that in September 1962 Arend Bouhuys of Holland, a well-known and respected investigator of byssinosis, was joining the faculty of Emory University in Atlanta. Bouhuy's adventures in Georgia will be the subject of our next chapter.

CONCLUSION

By 1962, progress finally seemed to be being made toward treating seriously the threat of byssinosis in the United States. Occupational health professionals in Georgia were on the lookout for the disease; they were publishing important articles on byssinosis, as were scholars elsewhere in the country. The Department of Health was showing some influence in the state legislature, and GTMA seemed to be very much on the defensive. But another ten to fifteen years of struggle lay ahead before byssinosis became the object of recognition, compensability, and standards.

The heroes in the story of the "mysterious disease" of byssinosis in Georgia are the occupational health specialists at the Department of Health such as Petrie, Dickson, McLean, and others. Levenstein and Tuminaro have suggested that "In the United States, the weakness of labor as a political and economic force," and this was certainly true in Georgia, "appears to be a critical influence on the regulation of occupational health." They conclude, then, that "The role of the public health scientist and advocate is of particular interest in this context" [12, p. 4].

The role of the public health scientists and advocates in Georgia cannot be overstressed. Yet in the end they were not able to launch any full-scale investigation into byssinosis, and the reason was lack of access—access to employee health records, when there were any, and access to the workplace. GTMA was by and large successful in blocking such access, and when a breach in the wall was threatened, as in the case of Bartow, Floyd, and Polk counties, GTMA did not hesitate to use its considerable influence and power to repair the damage.

Beardsley has written that,

> From the start the strategy of Southern mill owners when accused of harboring serious health hazards in their factories was either to ignore the charges, deflect them, or defame those who raised them [13, p. 207].

In the case of Georgia, Forbes and GTMA persisted in absolutely denying the existence of any signs of byssinosis in the mills, although they offered no evidence to support this contention. Their concerns seemed to be over any adverse effect a study of byssinosis would have on the public relations and industrial relations of the industry. Forbes feared a "mass hysteria" might overcome workers and that they would begin to imagine they had the symptoms of the disease. Overly zealous young doctors, "damage suit lawyers," and "governmental interference" were the culprits bringing unwanted and unneeded attention to the cotton textile industry. In the years ahead, similar charges, complaints, and strategies would be utilized by most, but not necessarily all, Southern mill owners.

ENDNOTES

1. Materials for this chapter are drawn primarily from Papers of the Georgia Textile Manufacturers Association (GTMA) obtained through the suit *Williams v. Lanier et al.* discussed in the previous chapter. We also draw on Georgia Department of Public Health (GDPH) papers obtained from the State of Georgia Archives in Atlanta.
2. Georgia Textile Manufacturers Association, *Health Evaluation of the Textile Worker in Georgia,* proposal to the National Institute of Health, appendix, Dickson *curriculum vitae.*
3. GTMA, T. M. Forbes, *Report of the Conference with Representatives . . .,* Georgia Textile Manufacturers Association, April 13, 1960. McLean interview.
4. Georgia Department of Public Health, State of Georgia Archives in Atlanta.
5. GTMA, T. M. Forbes, General Letter No. 6040: 4-22-60: *Proposed Study of Pulmonary and Respiratory Diseases Among Georgia Textile Industry Employees.*
6. GTMA, General Letter No. 6040.
7. See GDPH, Dickson to Petrie and McLean, 7/12/60. The initial article, "Pulmonary Disease and Cotton Processing," was co-authored by Dickson and McLean and published in December 1960 in the *Journal of the Medical Association of Georgia.*
8. GTMA, T. M. Forbes, General Letter No. 6067: 7-21-60: "Continued Interest in the Extent of Byssinosis Among Georgia Textile Mill Employees;" and GTMA, Forbes to McKenney, 7/18/60.
9. E. A. Shaptini, Byssinosis—A Review, *Industrial Medicine and Surgery, 30*:2, March 1961.
10. GTMA, T. M. Forbes, General Letter No. 6174: 5-17-61: "More About Byssinosis."
11. GTMA, T. M. Forbes, General Letter No. 6314: 8-24-62: "Industrial Air Pollution."
12. Charles Levenstein and Dominick J. Tuminaro, The Political Economy of Occupational Disease, in *Work, Health, and the Environment: Old Problems, New Solutions,* Charles Levenstein and John Wooding (eds.), The Guilford Press, New York, 1997.
13. Edward H. Beardsley, *A History of Neglect: Health Care for Black and Mill Workers in the Twentieth-Century South,* University of Tennessee Press, Knoxville, 1987.

CHAPTER 8

Bouhuys' Disease

PRELUDE

Ten minutes after Dr. Arend Bouhuys and a colleague inhaled a test spray of a saline extract of cotton dust, they quite suddenly felt a strangling tightness in their chests that lasted nearly the length of a working day. Listlessness accompanied this symptom.

The two researchers, working at a laboratory at the University of Lund, Sweden in 1958, had reproduced the acute byssinotic reaction to cotton dust that mill workers knew as "Monday morning feeling" and which occurred when the mill employees returned to the work environment after a weekend away. As Bouhuys described it,

> Dr. Lundin and I inhaled for 10 minutes a saline extract of cotton dust, which was aerosolized. The first ten minutes or so after the end of the inhalation we felt nothing particular, but then rather suddenly we developed a serious dyspnea [tightness in the chest], which lasted for at least six to eight hours, and which was accompanied by a general malaise.

The startled researchers repeated the experiment the next day, but they experienced no symptoms then, just as cotton mill workers in the early stages of the disease seemed to have no difficulty for the rest of the work week [1, Bouhuys to Schilling, 12/4/58].

DR. AREND BOUHUYS

Bouhuys was born in Deventer, the Netherlands in 1925. He received his medical education at the University of Utrecht, earning the MD in 1948, and did a residency in internal medicine at the University of Amsterdam. He became the Head of the Pulmonary Function Laboratory there in 1954. From 1955 to 1957 he was a resident in chest diseases at the University of Groningen. He was awarded a Ph.D. in Medical Sciences by the University of Amsterdam in 1956 for his dissertation on pneumotacography, a technique for measuring air flow in respiration. In 1959 he was appointed assistant professor of medicine and Head of the Laboratory of Clinical Physiology at the University of Leiden, where he remained until 1962. Bouhuys also traveled to Sweden frequently, serving as a summer research associate in the Department of Physiology at the University of Lund.

At Lund, Bouhuys had been working with S. E. Lindell on the effect of histamine on pulmonary ventilation when he first met R. S. F. Schilling in June of 1958. Schilling, drawing on the work of Prausnitz who two decades earlier had suggested that cotton dust might cause the liberation of histamines in the lungs, pointed out to Bouhuys a possible relationship between his histamine research and byssinosis. (Histamine is a compound released during an allergic reaction that causes dilation of capillaries, the contracting of smooth muscle, and other symptoms.)

That Fall Bouhuys started pursuing Schilling's lead, working with physiologists at Lund. They prepared extracts of mixed cotton dust and indeed discovered small amounts of histamine in the dust. But the levels were too low to affect even people who were highly sensitive. It was then that they tested their aerosolized extract and experienced the mill worker's Monday morning sensation. Bouhuys later wrote to Schilling:

> It is true that the symptoms after inhalation of this extract in our two human subjects are not the same as those found in byssinosis patients. As far as I can see, however, the main difference seems to be the different time course, i.e., the much slower reaction of byssinosis patients during their work hours [1, Bouhuys to Schilling, 1/2/59].

Soon after, Bouhuys colleagues in Sweden planned to test the histamine-liberation hypothesis in animal experiments and Bouhuys joined them in this work [1, Bouhuys to Schilling, 12/4/58]. A few months later, the animal experiments convinced the researchers that they had "fairly good evidence of a histamine-liberator in cotton dust." Schilling then invited Bouhuys to report on their progress at an April 1959 meeting of the British Medical Research Council's byssinosis committee [1, Bouhuys to Schilling, 1/2/59].

While in Great Britain, Bouhuys also visited a pneumoconiosis unit in Wales where he met with Gilson and McKerrow, two of Schilling's collaborators on byssinosis work. (McKerrow, it will be recalled, accompanied Schilling on a visit to the United States in 1960.) There they repeated the histamine inhalation experiment, this time with Gilson, McKerrow, and a technician as the subjects. The results were the same. In fact, Gilson subsequently was hospitalized with a flu-like condition, and his x-rays showed some peculiar markings which concerned McKerrow sufficiently that he wrote about it to Bouhuys [1, McKerrow to Bouhuys, 6/30/59]. Chest x-rays on McKerrow and the technician were normal, however, and Bouhuys doubted that Gilson would experience any lasting effects of the test unless it had aggravated a pre-existing bronchitis [1, Bouhuys to McKerrow, 7/15/59]. Clearly, though, the researchers were working on something both significant and dangerous.

Over the next two years or so, Bouhuys published at least a dozen papers related to histamine experiments and byssinosis in outlets ranging from the *British Medical Journal* to the *Journal of Psychology* to *La Medicina del Lavaro*. His collaborators and co-authors included Swedish and Dutch scientists as well as McKerrow. In 1961, he and Dr. Lindell presented their work in Paris at the 3rd World Congress on Prevention of Occupational Risks, and in 1962 Bouhuys hosted a meeting in Leiden of the International Union of Respiratory Physiologists [1, Bouhuys, *curriculum vitae*]. It was at this meeting that the American Wallace Fenn, head of the World Congress at that time, urged Bouhuys to consider working in the United States, a move that would enhance his career [2, Fenna Bouhuys interview, July 1983].

Soon after, Dr. Ross McLean, who had become familiar with Bouhuys' work, recruited him to Emory University, and in December Bouhuys was appointed Assistant Professor of Medicine and Assistant Professor of Physiology at Emory. Thus, in 1962 at the age of 37, the young but well-established researcher rented out his home in Holland and brought his family to Georgia [1, Fenna Bouhuys interview]. Bouhuys' adventures in the New World would bring him both great frustration and great success.

BOUHUYS IN GEORGIA

In April of 1962, McLean wrote to Bouhuys that the American Thoracic Society had awarded him a grant to continue his research studies [1, McLean to Bouhuys, 4/11/62]. McLean decided to no longer pursue byssinosis-related research, as with the recognized expert in this field now on board at Emory he could return to his clinical activities [1, Hurst to Bouhuys, 6/15/62; McLean interview, 6/16/83].

Bouhuys also applied to the U.S. Public Health Service for funding to continue research on the impact of cotton dust on lung tissue. The USPHS turned down this request but suggested he conduct an epidemiological investigation to determine whether byssinosis was a problem in the United States. Funding for this study was then provided. This was precisely the kind of study for which Dickson, McLean, and Orr had sought funding and the support of the Georgia Textile Manufacturers Association, and precisely the kind of study that Ted Forbes and GTMA had labored so strenuously and successfully to thwart.

Predictably, announcement of the federal grant to Bouhuys brought a strong and prompt reaction from Forbes and the owners association, echoing their response to the earlier research team. Forbes wrote to the President of Emory University about the study:

The Georgia textile manufacturing industry has been damaged, in the eyes of the public, I think, by a recent Atlanta newspaper story [see 1, McLean to Bouhuys, 4/11/62] that was based upon some statements that were said to have been made by one Arend Bouhuys. . . . If such a high incidence of any disease, as that claimed by your professor with respect to "byssinosis" existed in Georgia's largest industry, surely that fact would long since have been discovered and corrective action would have been required. . . . On more than one past occasion the alleged existence of "byssinosis" in cotton textile plants has been used as an excuse for inaugurating some research project. . . . But in all of these instances preliminary studies have shown that there is no factual basis for claiming that there is a high incidence, or even a slight existence, of this mysterious malady among Georgia textile employees [2, Forbes to Atwood, 6/2/64].

Forbes then circulated this letter among GTMA members along with the following prescription:

We remind you that this will be a private investigation by a private education institution. Therefore, your participation would be purely voluntary on your part. There will be no legal or governmental compulsion in the survey [3].

As a result of Forbes' campaign, Bouhuys was unable to gain access to a single privately owned mill in Georgia. Yet Bouhuys was resourceful and determined, and gained permission to conduct an epidemiological study at a fairly modern cotton mill in the federal penitentiary in Atlanta. The results of this study would later play a significant role in Bouhuys' marshaling of evidence for the existence of byssinosis in the United States.

To say the least, Bouhuys must have found the hostile research climate among Georgia textile manufacturers discouraging and frustrating. Still, he persevered and remained alert for any opportunities to do field studies on byssinosis. One such opportunity seemed to present itself when Bouhuys read a report in the *American Review of Respiratory Disease* that Dr. Kay Kilburn, then at the Veterans Administration hospital in Durham, North Carolina, and Dr. Leo J. Heaphy, Assistant Professor of Medicine at Bourman-Gray School of Medicine in Greensboro, were interested in byssinosis. He wrote to Heaphy:

I have been trying, so far unsuccessfully, to find an opportunity for a survey in industry, and I am wondering whether you would be willing to cooperate in such a study, if it proves feasible [1, Bouhuys to Heaphy, 7/29/64].

Although they were not able to gain access to a plant at the time, Bouhuys and Heaphy continued to correspond and Heaphy was to become an important collaborator with Bouhuys.

ON TO YALE

Bouhuys also received moral and some small financial support from his friends and colleagues in Europe. In October 1963 Schilling returned to Emory to give a talk on "Byssinosis in Textile Workers." He then went up to New Haven, Connecticut, and wrote to Bouhuys suggesting that he should meet two British-born professors at Yale, one of whom was the head of the Department of Epidemiology and Public Health [1, Schilling to Bouhuys, 10/24/63]. Bouhuys later replied to Schilling, thanking him for a $1000 grant from the World Health Organization for byssinosis research [1, Bouhuys to Schilling, 12/5/63]. By the summer of 1964, the contacts in New Haven had developed into an offer of a new position. In August, Bouhuys informed Emory University that he would be resigning as of December 1. He would be moving to Connecticut to take up a position as Associate Professor at Yale Medical School and Fellow of the John B. Pierce Foundation Laboratory [1, Bouhuys to Brecker, 8/31/64]. The peripatetic pace of Bouhuys' career, family life, and research would continue.

At Yale, Bouhuys remained in contact with Heaphy. In June 1965, for instance, Bouhuys visited Heaphy in Durham and later wrote to him about their discussions:

> I know that you feel the diagnosis should include function tests before and after work on Monday and other days, and I agree with that, a paper based on the histories you obtained and the pulmonary function data which you have would be a breakthrough in the history of byssinosis! [1, Bouhuys to Heaphy, 6/28/65].

This breakthrough would begin to come together in late 1965. Dr. Irving Selikoff, then Chairman of the New York Academy of Science's Division of Environmental Sciences, asked Bouhuys to give a talk on byssinosis to the Academy. Bouhuys immediately contacted Heaphy, noting that Selikoff had specifically asked him to include material on the prevalence of byssinosis in the United States, as Dr. Harriet Hardy, a pioneering occupational health physician based in Boston, "had just told him a week ago that it did not exist here at all!" [1, Bouhuys to Heaphy, 11/4/65].

Bouhuys also wrote to Ross McLean, who was still at Emory, explaining Selikoff's request and asking him for data on the patients he had seen. Bouhuys' enthusiasm and optimism were clear:

> From your and Leo Heaphy's experiences together, it should be obvious that there is byssinosis in the U.S. and that epidemiological studies are needed. If you know about anybody else who may have experience with byssinosis in the South, I would appreciate you letting me know [1, Bouhuys to McLean, 11/4/65].

Heaphy shared Bouhuys' mood. Upon sending the data on his patients to Bouhuys, he remarked:

> I certainly hope that you can use this material and Ross McLean's data to convince the non-believers that this entity does exist and is a real problem in American textile mills [1, Heaphy to Bouhuys, 12/30/65].

Bouhuys' talk before the New York Academy of Sciences was published in the Academy's journal *Transactions* [4]. It was well-received, but of course much remained to be done.

Even as Bouhuys collected American byssinosis cases and searched for an opportunity to do an industry survey, his experimental work with cotton dust continued at Yale. This to McLean:

> We found that the histamine-releasing agent in cotton dust derives from the bracts, small leaves around the stem of the boll. An extract of bracts releases histamine in human lung tissue in vitro [in the environment] and also causes dyspnea and mechanical changes after inhalation in vivo [in the body] [1, Bouhuys to McLean, 11/4/65].

Some of the laboratory work involved analysis of urine collected from hemp workers in Spain to determine the presence of histamine metabolites, comparing Monday morning excretions with those of other days [1, Bouhuys to McLean, 11/4/65]. In 1964 Bouhuys had proposed to Dr. Antonio Barbero Carnicero a study of byssinosis in Spain in a rural setting where there would be no complications from air pollution [1, Bouhuys to Barbero, 1/15/64]. Preliminary work was done in a hemp mill near Alicante, Spain. Eventually, several publications came out of this work on which Swedish and British investigators also collaborated [5]. Some years later Bouhuys wrote to Barbero about the importance of these studies:

> The studies with you in Collasa de Segura have led to very extensive studies in different towns in the U.S., over the years 1972-1978, including a large study of cotton textile workers in South Carolina, but it is hard to get something useful done [1, Bouhuys to Barbero, 1/21/79].

RECOGNITION

The byssinosis case collection effort went slowly. But a Dutch colleague, Dr. Johannes A. Kylstra, who was teaching at Duke University Medical Center, provided information to Bouhuys on one byssinosis patient, and, more importantly, contacted Dr. Kay Kilburn, who had become Chief of Medicine for the Veteran's Administration, on Bouhuys' behalf. The idea was for Kilburn to open the records of VA patients to Bouhuys [1, Kylstra to Bouhuys, 11/30/66]. Kilburn had studied textile workers in the past with Heaphy and he was willing to cooperate, although he told Bouhuys,

> My own feeling is that byssinosis is not a disease but a type of hypersensitivity in people who are within the asthmatic category. Their exposure to the

products in cotton mill dust thus acts in a non-specific manner. I agree that to demonstrate the importance an industrial survey is needed [1, Kilburn to Bouhuys, 12/16/66].

Kilburn was well aware of the difficulties in gaining access to industry. In the past, VA staff had been unable to get any cooperation from industry for a survey. In the past year, however, limited cooperation had come at an Erwin Mill plant and Derwin Cooper, a VA physician, had some preliminary data. As Kilburn summarized,

> Last year we attempted one [industrial survey] at the Erwin plant in Durham but were not permitted to interview patients or to test them. They did, however, have x-rays and answered a three question card about the presence of shortness of breath, cough and sputum production.

Kilburn also expressed his concern that all except one of the workers surveyed were smokers, a fact that tended to obscure the cause of their problems and made it more difficult to establish the industrial nature of the disease [1, Kilburn to Bouhuys, 12/16/66].

By 1967, Bouhuys had assembled a scientific paper which reported on a group of 22 cotton textile workers from three Southern states, and which provided clinical evidence of byssinosis in the United States. "Byssinosis in the United States" was published in the prestigious *New England Journal of Medicine* under the authorship of Bouhuys, Heaphy, Schilling, and another researcher named Welborn. Kilburn was acknowledged for "allowing us to see three patients at the Department of Medicine, Veterans Administration Hospital, Durham, North Carolina." The authors urged that epidemiological studies be undertaken to ascertain the prevalence of the disease:

> The present study shows that disabling byssinosis occurs in the United States, and suggests that hundreds among the 200,000 or more cotton-production workers in this country may suffer from byssinosis in its early as well as in its late stages. Whenever a few patients with byssinosis have been identified by physicians, in other parts of the world, and this observation was followed up in epidemiologic studies, many more workers similarly affected have been identified [6, p. 174].

The paper received a strong and positive reaction. Numerous requests were coming in for reprints of the article [1, Moulton to Bouhuys, 8/4/67]. Schilling was particularly pleased that the *New England Journal* had accepted the article:

> I would like reprints as soon as possible if I may, because I have mentioned it to the Textile Worker's Union here, and they are going to take up the whole problem of byssinosis in the United States with colleagues in the U.S. . . . [1, Schilling to Bouhuys, 5/10/67].

The research pace began to pick up. In September, Welborn informed Bouhuys that he was making arrangements for them to conduct a plant survey at

Mayfair Mill in Arcadia, South Carolina, and the two made plans to do so in December [1, Wilborn to Dent, 9/5/67; Bouhuys to Welborn, 11/15/67]. Funding also had come through for an international conference on byssinosis in Alicante, Spain. Finally, by the end of the year, results were coming in from Bouhuys' collaborator, Wolfson, at the Atlanta penitentiary mill: 27 percent of 85 workers in the prison mill had byssinosis, mostly the reversible Grade I version of the disease [1, Bouhuys to Schilling, 12/1/67].

Yet while Bouhuys was at last making progress on industrial surveys, his academic career seemed to be in trouble. Up for promotion to full professor in the Department of Medicine at Yale, he became convinced by May 1967, as he wrote to Schilling, that ". . . apparently . . . they do not want me after all." He added, ". . . They probably prefer someone who is not interested in such controversial matters as byssinosis" [1, Bouhuys to Schilling, 5/10/67]. Schilling commiserated, and suggested,

> I think you are right that the main thing is to get a lot of good work done in the next two years, you will have no difficulty at all in getting opportunities for continuing your research elsewhere, the only problem is moving with a family [1, Schilling to Bouhuys, 5/10/67].

In mid-December, however, Bouhuys wrote to his friend Schilling with good news: Yale had offered him the Professorship in Medicine after all [1, Bouhuys to Schilling, 12/18/67]. Schilling sent his congratulations: "It means you have been recognized" [1, Schilling to Bouhuys, 1/5/68].

By 1968, Bouhuys and his colleagues had established that byssinosis as a clinical entity was present in the United States. By 1969, his epidemiological studies confirmed that the problem was not rare. Bouhuys' numerous articles appeared in a variety of well-respected peer reviewed journals, and no *scientific* controversy arose over his findings. Bouhuys and byssinosis had come to recognition in the United States at the same time.

AFTERWORD

The arrival of Dr. Bouhuys in the United States in the early sixties did not open a new period in byssinosis research. Rather, his work represents the culmination and fruition of efforts toward serious investigation of byssinosis in the United States that had been building throughout the 1950s. One need only look back at the efforts of Petrie, Dickson, Venable, McLean, Orr, and their colleagues, as well as the later work of Bouhuys' collaborators such as Heaphy and Welborn. It might also be recalled the excitement caused by Schilling and McKerrow's 1960 lecture on byssinosis: "The young doctors who were present seemed fascinated by the discussion . . ." (see Chapter 7).

In our view, such momentum cannot be separated from the more general stirrings of social activity and social concern that were emerging at the same time and would soon grow to challenge all the major institutions of the United States.

First and foremost among this activism was the Civil Rights Movement of the 1950s and 1960s. Its appearance challenged the South in ways it had never before been challenged, and also, as has been said, was a "borning struggle" to the activism that would soon engulf the nation. Many of those who participated in the Civil Rights Movement went on to make their voices heard in other movements, including the struggle for worker health and safety.

Early in this period in the South, there was little increase in working class activity in the conventional sense of a trade union movement. In fact, as we will later discuss, organized labor in the textile industry came late to byssinosis as an issue of concern. The complaints coming in to the Georgia Department of Public Health did not appear to be part of any organized effort to raise the cotton dust issue. Still, it seems probable that textile workers were beginning in larger numbers to dare to complain about the conditions of their work, in an unorganized but persistent effort to improve them. In addition, these were "good times" for Southern textiles—sales and profits continued to grow. In such periods, management may become more attentive to labor conditions, particularly if job slots are getting harder to fill, and workers can take more risks when jobs are plentiful.

In the midst of this simmering social brew, one of the most important ingredients was that health care professionals were listening to the concerns of textile workers, were growing impatient with the stalling and intransigence of the industry, and were slowly building evidence that byssinosis was disabling and killing these workers.

As with the banning of the suck shuttle in Massachusetts in the early part of the century, then, a convergence of historical forces was coming together—albeit forces different in many ways from the earlier period—that would lead to significant change. In this case, the change would be the recognition of byssinosis as a compensable occupational disease. But, much frustration and struggle still lay ahead.

ENDNOTES

1. Archives at Sterling Library (ASL), Yale University. Most of the materials for this chapter are drawn from this source. In addition, Mrs. Fenna Bouhuys was kind enough to grant Charles Levenstein an interview and provide him with her late husband's *curriculum vitae.*
2. Georgia Textile Manufacturers Association.
3. Georgia Textile Manufacturers Association, T. M. Forbes, General Letter No. 6522: 6-4-64.

4. Arend Bouhuys, Byssinosis in Textile Workers, *Transactions, 28,* pp. 480-490, 1966.
5. See, for instance, Arend Bouhuys et al., Byssinosis in Hemp Workers, *Archives of Environment and Health, 14,* pp. 533-544, 1967.
6. Arend Bouhuys et al., Byssinosis in the United States, *New England Journal of Medicine,* July 1967.

CHAPTER 9

Brown Lung and the Dilemmas of a Novice Investigator, 1968-1969

In the late 1960s, a research collaboration between two young doctors in North Carolina led to a storm of controversy and eventually helped move the plight of byssinotic textile workers onto the national stage. Bouhuys was brought into the fray, in support of these two physicians, one in particular, who together had succeeded in doing what Bouhuys himself had found so terribly difficult—gaining access to a mill to study the health of workers.

THE PLAYERS

After graduating from Harvard Medical School, Dr. Peter Schrag, like many young physicians of his generation, decided to serve in the United States Public Health Service rather than go to Vietnam. This he did from 1966 to 1968, becoming an officer of the Epidemiological Intelligence Service. He was assigned to the North Carolina Department of Health and worked as an epidemiologist under Dr. Martin Hines, head of the Department's Epidemiology Division. Schrag has recalled that during his time in North Carolina he read and was influenced by W. J. Cash's classic work *The Mind of the South* [1] and its depiction of the rise of the textile industry in the state and its centrality to the state's economy [2]. Schrag's personal interest in North Carolina's textile industry would soon intersect with his professional duties as an epidemiologist.

At the same time as Schrag was working for North Carolina's Department of Public Health, Dr. A. Dale Gullett was serving as company physician for Fieldcrest Mills headquartered in Raleigh. Gullett had joined Fieldcrest in 1964 after having completed a residency in occupational medicine at UCLA. When he was applying for the job at Fieldcrest's Eden, North Carolina mill, Gullett indicated an interest in doing studies of byssinosis and even asked to see the Eden mill's card room. From his observations, Gullett later noted, he believed there was indeed a cotton dust problem at the mill—and, by extension, at other Fieldcrest mills, but he also believed the company was genuinely unaware of the problem [3].

It in fact would have been difficult for Fieldcrest to be aware of the extent of the problem, as until Gullett's hiring the company had no medical department as such, although there was one nurse for the company's several plants. There were no industrial hygienists on the payroll. On the other hand, Fieldcrest, or at least some key executives of the firm, indicated to Gullett its own interest in conducting byssinosis studies [3]. That this was so is backed up by the simple fact that Fieldcrest did indeed hire Gullett, who had made no secret of his concerns with byssinosis. By way of contrast, one can only imagine how, say, Ted Forbes of the GTMA (see the previous two chapters) would have reacted to Gullett.

Unfortunately, yet almost predictably given the labyrinthine nature of the story of byssinosis so far, shortly after Gullett came on board the executive who had hired him and had been the most sympathetic to card room dust problems at Fieldcrest left the company. This delayed but did not deter Gullett's efforts.

Gullett would, for instance, often contact the North Carolina Department of Health for advice on questions of industrial hygiene, and also frequently talk with Department hygienist John Lumsden about doing a byssinosis study. Gullett felt Lumsden, who would later work with Dr. James Merchant on important investigations at Burlington Mills (see Chapter 10), certainly was knowledgeable about byssinosis but lacked access to plants in order to conduct any serious studies. Between 1964 and 1967 Gullett spoke regularly with other physicians in the industry about the cotton dust problem, many of whom advised him not even to attempt to do a study of byssinosis. Gullett also was aware of the Georgia Textile Manufacturers Association's reaction to Arend Bouhuys' attempts to get into the mills in Georgia. He had seen a copy of the memo GTMA had circulated to its membership warning about Bouhuys [3]. In sum, Gullett was hardly naive when it came to the politics of byssinosis within the textile industry.

Nevertheless, the times were changing. Social activism, as we discussed in the previous chapter, was on the rise. Bouhuys' work was beginning to bear fruit. Byssinosis was on the agenda. Gullett reported that in 1966 or 1967 an industry conference was held on the issue but never publicized [3]. North Carolina manufacturers, though powerful, did not have the clout GTMA had in Georgia. Gullett had been hired by Fairchild knowing full well his intentions to investigate byssinosis [4]. And Gullett—an insider, a *company* doctor—pushed, working hard to convince managers, who feared they might be forced to close mills, that such a study was in fact desirable. In 1967, Gullett began making arrangements to do a study of byssinosis at Fieldcrest. It is at this point he came into contact with Schrag [3].

As part of his duties in the Epidemiology Division, Schrag negotiated the agreement with Fieldcrest to carry out a study at one of its mills. Schrag agreed ". . . not to publish or publicize the results of a study done at Fieldcrest Mills, Inc., without first obtaining written approval from the company." He also agreed not to identify Fieldcrest Mills, "[s]ince byssinosis is not a problem unique to Fieldcrest Mills" [5].

Despite such assurances, the collaborative study by Schrag and Gullett was postponed several times. Finally, however, in February 1968 the survey was completed [3]. After completion of this field research, Schrag's term of service with the USPHS ended and he left for New York City to do a residency at Harlem Hospital. Gullett left Fieldcrest in 1968.

THE BROUHAHA BEGINS

Schrag was eager to make something of the research he and Gullett had done, for the results had been impressive. Schrag and Gullett had indeed found byssinosis among the 509 Fieldcrest workers they studied. Sixty-three workers were diagnosed with the disease, though only 20 of them had the most serious form of it—Stage III—which produced the breathlessness and often chest tightness all week long while they worked [6].

By July 1968, Schrag had finished a draft of an article which he sent to George Moore, President of Fieldcrest. He attached a note to the article, asking for Moore's comments before publication and stating, in part,

> I am convinced the subject [byssinosis] should be brought to the attention of the medical profession . . . I . . . would now like to publish the enclosed paper in the *New England Journal of Medicine*. I recall you agreed that the results of our studies in Leaksville could be included in publication so long as there would be no identification or reference either to North Carolina or Fieldcrest Mills [5, Schrag to Moore, 7/30/68].

Moore took nearly two months two reply. He explained that Gullett's replacement at Fieldcrest was still going through orientation and that,

> Until such time and until we have had an opportunity to confirm the results of your study and take the indicated personnel actions, we feel it would be inadvisable to agree to publication or publicity in any form [5, Moore to Schrag, 9/26/68].

Schrag got the hint; it was clear any agreement to publish from Fieldcrest would not soon be forthcoming. Thus, Schrag contacted his former colleagues at the North Carolina Health Department, detailing his problems with Fieldcrest. Here too, however, he was asked not to publish the paper:

> . . . we are on the threshold of another breakthrough in this area and publication of your paper at this time, against Mr. Moore's wishes, might place the state Board of Health in an embarrassing position [5, Hines to Schrag, 10/8/68].

After this rather cryptic rebuff, Schrag next wrote to the federal office under whose auspices he had worked in North Carolina—the Communicable Disease Center's State Services Section. Explaining that he had "had to sign a release" in order to carry out the study, Schrag asked if the U.S. Department of Health, Education and Welfare would "put pressure on the company and persuade it to give me permission to publish this study." Since byssinosis was a problem throughout the textile states, he reasoned HEW would have a legitimate interest in the matter and, apparently, some jurisdictional clout.

If the federal government was not willing to pressure Fieldcrest or if it was willing but unsuccessful in its efforts, Schrag asked that the agency allow him to identify himself as an Epidemiological Intelligence Service Officer and publish the study without Fieldcrest's permission. This course of action was legally safe, according to a lawyer Schrag had consulted. Finally, Schrag wrote that if the agency would not or could not go along with his request, he and his co-author Gullett might publish the paper independently or turn the research results over "to someone like Ralph Nader," who by this time had firmly established himself as a corporate gadfly and major opinion leader in the country. Schrag was not only convinced that Fieldcrest intended to suppress the results of the byssinosis study, but also that the head of the company "plans to fire all byssinotic employees and says so euphemistically" [5, Schrag to Conrad and Witte, 10/19/68]. Schrag's impatience and sense of urgency as he tried to bring the study to the light of day are thus quite understandable.

The man who had been Schrag's immediate supervisor in the Epidemiological Intelligence Service, Dr. John Witte, the head of the State Services Section, turned Schrag's letter over to the highly respected Dr. Alexander Langmuir, chief of epidemiology for the National Communicable Disease Center in Atlanta. Langmuir reviewed the issues raised in Schrag's requests and addressed eight points in his response. These points are worth looking at in some detail, as, on the whole, they tend to form an honest and straightforward appraisal of the pitfalls, stumbling blocks, and barricades occupational health investigators often face, especially if they are not yet well-established in their field.

First and foremost, Langmuir noted, "The study should be published."

Second, though the issue of byssinosis was certainly of national importance, nonetheless no real interstate issue was involved. The Center had no jurisdictional right to pressure either Fieldcrest or the North Carolina State Health Department. "We could, however, use our not inconsiderable powers of persuasion," Langmuir added.

Third, the paper did in fact need approval at the state level: "We certainly cannot approve or clear publication without the prior clearance from the State Health Officer." Further,

> Peter [Schrag] would be foolhardy to attempt publication without identification. I doubt if a reputable journal would accept the paper and sooner or later the identification would leak out.

Fourth, Langmuir cautioned Schrag that his professional reputation was at stake. Schrag, after all, was not forced to sign the release: "this [the signing] sounds like compulsion whereas it apparently was a voluntary contract." Schrag might think of himself as a martyr, but ". . . professionally he will be known as a man who doesn't keep his word."

Fifth, the paper needed substantial editing, not for substance, but to tighten it up and make it a "lucid, short, wholly persuasive paper. . . ."

Sixth, after editing, "every effort should be made through Martin Hines to persuade Fieldcrest Mills to reverse their present position." And, "careful circulation" of the unpublished paper to public health and industry leaders might help.

Langmuir's seventh point addressed the public health purposes involved in Schrag's work, and criticized Schrag's threat to take the information to "someone like Ralph Nader."

> The essential constructive step from the public health point of view is persuading the textile industry to face reality and take the necessary corrective steps. I believe these are better taken through official channels than by sensational popular articles in magazines and newspapers. While the latter often achieve action, I doubt that Pete Schrag wants to follow that path in his professional career.

In his final point, Langmuir suggested that byssinosis might be "a subject for major attention" at the new federal research center under construction near Raleigh and Durham.

He concluded by reiterating that Schrag should proceed through normal channels and seek support from the North Carolina State Health Department. "I am afraid that Pete will consider me an old and experienced buck passer, but I have tried to be constructive . . ." [5, Langmuir to Witte, 10/21/68].

The long message from Langmuir was passed along to Schrag through Witte, who added his own letter after talking with Martin Hines in North Carolina. Hines indicated that his problem with the Schrag and Gullett article was only one of timing. At the moment, the Department of Health was working on a major legislative effort on occupational health in the state and wanted no distraction from that. But after March 1969 this effort would be over and the Health Department would be free to proceed. Hines said he had talked to Schrag about all of this, and that he had been under the impression that Schrag had understood and accepted the delay. Accordingly, Witte wrote to Schrag,

> I would suggest that you take another look at the paper . . . and work on a new draft with Martin Hines. When you and Martin then have a paper that you both feel happy with, forward it to Atlanta and we will see that the appropriate clearances are instituted. With Martin's support and endorsement of a very good manuscript, I would anticipate no difficulty in [Center] clearance [5, Witte to Schrag, 11/5/68].

Schrag quickly responded to Witte. He was not unwilling to work with Hines on a revision of the paper, he said, but both Hines and Dr. Jacob Koomen, the Director of the North Carolina State Board of Health,

> have made it clear to me that the North Carolina State Board of Health cannot publish an article on byssinosis and will not be openly associated with any efforts to criticize the textile industry.

Because of this stance, Schrag thought Witte's plan was "unrealistic" and he urged the Communicable Disease Center to try to bring industry around [5, Schrag to Witte, 11/11/68].

Witte was frustrated by Schrag's response. To him, the problem in North Carolina was indeed one of delay, not of suppression. He thus reassured Schrag, in what was becoming a Ping-Pong match of correspondence between the two, that "Martin expressed a willingness to work with you and feels that your paper should be published" [5, Witte to Schrag, 11/18/68].

In his return, Schrag wrote that he hoped Witte's impression was correct. He also noted his willingness to postpone publication of the paper if that would help passage of occupational health legislation in North Carolina and that he had in fact indicated this to Hines. But to Schrag the problem was not simply "one of timing." The fact was, he stressed, that ". . . I cannot publish without a legal release from the company." Hines was unwilling to ask Fieldcrest to reverse its position, and apparently Schrag had little faith that Hines would be willing to do so in the future. Accordingly, Schrag once again asked for federal help:

> A letter from an official of the Department of Health, Education and Welfare expressing awareness and interest in our results and appealing to Fieldcrest's better instincts would be most helpful [5, Schrag to Witte, 11/21/68].

No doubt tiring of the game, Witte acceded to Schrag's request and wrote to Fieldcrest's President, G. William Moore, urging him to permit publication of the paper due to its scientific importance. He assured Moore that Schrag would submit a final draft to Fieldcrest for approval prior to submitting it to a journal [5, Witte to Moore, 11/27/68].

Haven Newton, Fieldcrest's Divisional Vice-President for Industrial Relations, responded to Witte on behalf of Moore. He enclosed a copy of Schrag's original agreement and reiterated the company's objections to publication. The reply has the alarmist, obfuscatory, and vaguely threatening tone we have already seen in so much of the textile industry response to anything having to do with byssinosis:

> You can appreciate the potential employee misunderstanding inherent in premature publicity. We feel strongly about the necessity for taking certain personnel actions before any such possibility exists. We must hold Dr. Schrag and others to our original understanding until this situation changes [5, Newton to Witte, 12/5/68].

In other words, there was no way Fieldcrest was going to grant Schrag permission to publish, and so things seemed to be at an impasse. This changed, however—in a turn of events that would not be believable in a work of fiction—due to a simple bureaucratic error.

LIGHT OF DAY

Schrag was hopeful that at least at some point in time he would be able to publish the study; in order to get a head start on the process of CDC clearance, he submitted a draft to Frances Porscher of Langmuir's staff. Then, according to Schrag,

> Miss Frances Porscher (sic) . . . abstracted my paper without my knowledge or permission and obviously without consulting the North Carolina State Board of Health and distributed it throughout the country in a CDC publication describing forthcoming papers [5, Schrag to Langmuir, 2/15/69].

To make matters worse, the report was noticed ". . . by a man interested in consumer protection who spoke in North Carolina, used my data, and made the local papers." Hines saw the newspaper article and called it to Schrag's attention, to Schrag's "considerable embarrassment." More significantly, Arend Bouhuys also saw the abstract and contacted Schrag. Bouhuys invited Schrag to Yale, and the two reviewed the Fieldcrest study as well as Schrag's dilemma [5, Schrag to Langmuir, 2/15/69; Bouhuys to Langmuir, 1/24/69].

Convinced of the value of Schrag's study, Bouhuys jumped into the publishing controversy, writing to Langmuir and urging him to use his influence to obtain permission from Fieldcrest to publish the work:

> I have reviewed Dr. Schrag's manuscript and find it a very interesting study. I believe he has used appropriate methods and has come to scientifically acceptable conclusions. . . . Our experience with byssinosis in this country, which to date is based on the study of about 400 cotton mill workers in three different mills, fully supports Dr. Schrag's findings.

Bouhuys explained that in his own case he had promised to send his papers to management of the mills where he conducted research—two were commercial and the third was the Atlanta penitentiary mill—but that "publication of our papers is in no way dependent upon the consent of these mill owners." He went on to argue that when two different sets of investigators came to similar conclusions as a result of independent studies, it was most important that they both publish. The abstract was already in the public domain anyway, and the Assistant Attorney General, Charles Johnson, had incorporated information from the abstract in a speech he had given in Atlanta on environmental problems in the South. Bouhuys also suggested Langmuir let Fieldcrest know that the Bouhuys' research team had two papers near completion on byssinosis and that the mills would not be identified.

Fieldcrest might as well capitulate; it had very little to lose from publication of the Schrag paper.

Perhaps the most intriguing element in Bouhuys argument was his appeal to Langmuir's professionalism, and the differences in the approach to public health between the two the appeal highlights. To Langmuir, it will be recalled, the "public health purposes" of Schrag's study would best be served if he went through "official channels," in that way "persuading the textile industry to . . . take the necessary corrective steps." Bouhuys, on the other hand, while not dismissing "official channels," certainly does not hold them sacrosanct either. Yes, it was indeed unfortunate that Schrag had signed the agreement with Fieldcrest. Nevertheless,

> . . . as a medical investigator who has performed a study supported by public funds, he has the duty to publish findings which clearly relate to the health of a significant segment of the American population, so that the medical profession in this country will become aware of his findings and their implications [5, Bouhuys to Langmuir, 1/24/69].

As in so many other arenas during the 1960s, here caution and procedural correctness confront, if not insurgency, certainly an impatience with this inherently conservative approach. The differences between the two "sides" would not soon be reconciled, but in the end impatience would serve the victims of byssinosis well.

Schrag again wrote to Fieldcrest in February 1969. He asked permission to present the paper at the spring meeting of the American Thoracic Society. His paper, he said, would be one of "several" given on the topic of byssinosis. He added that the "indicated personnel actions" the company had said it wished to take would surely have been performed by now, as it had been almost a year since the Fieldcrest workers had been studied. "As a physician," Schrag wrote, "I cannot cooperate in the suppression indefinitely of medical information" [5, Schrag to Moore, 2/7/69]. A copy of the letter was sent to John Witte.

On the same day Schrag wrote to Fieldcrest, Witte wrote to Schrag that he had learned of Schrag's planned American Thoracic Society presentation and that he was "very distressed" by this news. He had talked with Dr. Langmuir, and they had agreed on a proper course of action:

> This is clearly a breach of a written agreement that you have with the textile manufacturer involved. Unless you can receive their written approval to present your findings to the American Thoracic Society, I believe strongly that you must request that your paper be removed from the program and that the abstract not be published. [Witte was obviously unaware it already had been.] In order to retain your professional integrity and scientific reputation, I see no alternative [5, Witte to Schrag, 2/7/69].

Witte was now playing hard ball; references to "professional integrity" and "scientific reputation" are to a young researcher trying to establish a career not-so-veiled threats. Unfortunately, Langmuir joined in on the intimidation.

Langmuir had delivered a reply to Bouhuys' letter and sent a copy to Schrag. He had discussed the Fieldcrest situation with Witte and Kooman, head of the North Carolina Department of Health, and they had come to the conclusion that there was nothing to be done. Schrag had committed himself to obtain a release from the company and without it he should not speak or publish on the byssinosis study. Langmuir went even further in his cautions: "Frankly, this should include not talking about his work before a group of students or other individuals in view of the very strong feelings of Fieldcrest Mills." He requested Bouhuys intervene with Schrag and dissuade him from violating the agreement. "Schrag's reputation as a man of honesty and integrity is more important than his publicizing this one study." On the copy that he sent to Schrag, Langmuir hand wrote the following note:

> Dear Peter,
> The letter is written with due deliberation of the total situation. I hope you will change from your suicidal course [5, Langmuir to Bouhuys, 2/12/69].

Schrag had had enough. His reply to Langmuir was swift and angry. The only help he had gotten in his effort to persuade Fieldcrest to permit publication was Witte's one letter.

> You insist that my obligation to abide by a written agreement made before the study was begun is paramount. You do not mention my obligation, as well as yours and Dr. Kooman's, to see to it that information I obtained is not used to the detriment of the employees of Fieldcrest Mills. . . . I have . . . been advised by the former plant physician of Fieldcrest Mills, who is the co-author of my paper, that the management plans to fire all byssinotic employees and to replace them with young men who are kept unaware of the hazards inherent in their work. I am unwilling, despite your strenuous urging, to be the management's accomplice.

Fieldcrest's refusal to permit him to speak at the American Thoracic Society meeting more than a year after the study was done was unacceptable. Echoing Bouhuys' insistence on an overriding public health ethic, Schrag declared that, "Public Health officials who discover epidemics are obligated to institute preventive and educational measures." He then repeated his threat to seek wider publicity for the issue:

> If my latest request for a release from Fieldcrest is denied, I shall be forced to seek the legal advice of Mr. Ralph Nader who is interested in occupational health and can possibly advise me as to the merits of my case and the best way to protect myself and the employees of Fieldcrest Mills.

Copies of the letter were sent to Bouhuys and Koomen [5, Schrag to Langmuir, 2/15/69].

Ten days later, Fieldcrest agreed to the publication of Schrag's study. Haven Newton confirmed the agreement in writing, with the understanding that the company would not be identified in the report. "From my point of view," wrote Newton, "it would be a minor tragedy if one company, having taken a positive step in this matter, should be unfairly singled out for criticism" [5, Newton to Schrag, 2/25/69].

Witte was pleased with the news and promised Schrag he would let Langmuir know. Schrag could, of course, be identified as "formerly Epidemiological Intelligence Service Officer assigned to the North Carolina State Board of Health," though the ever cautious Witte thought this too should be cleared with Hines, especially if state officials would be listed as co-authors or acknowledged in some way [5, Witte to Schrag, 2/25/69].

The final issue to be negotiated among Schrag, Newton, Kooman, and Hines was the release to Fieldcrest of the names of the 63 byssinotic workers identified in the study. In April, Kooman wrote to Schrag and summed up the resolution of the situation. He asked Schrag to send to Newton ". . . the names of the twenty individuals who from your studies appear to be most seriously affected with byssinosis."

> Mr. Newton and I feel this will permit putting these individuals under proper surveillance and thereby making it possible to provide high-level medical care to each. Where necessary, Mr. Newton will be responsible for re-evaluation as to job placement so that each may be placed in his plant where best determined for reasons of health.

Koomen then added,

> We're pleased that Mr. Newton has agreed to release you from your earlier agreement. . . . We're pleased too with the intensity of his interest in follow-up of those who have chest problems so that they may be well situated and well cared for [5, Koomen to Schrag, 4/4/69].

Schrag sent the list of names a few days later. He told Newton he hoped the company would indeed find ways to transfer within the firm the workers who were disabled by byssinosis. Schrag seemed to be offering a not-so-subtle dig at the born-again sincerity of Fieldcrest (and perhaps that of others who had done so little to help Schrag's work see the light of day) by mimicking Newton's phrasing from the letter quoted above:

> From my point of view, it would be a major tragedy if the information I obtained was ever used contrary to the best interests of these workers who cooperated in good faith with the state health department [5, Schrag to Newton, 4/10/69].

CONCLUSION

The Fieldcrest study was conceived by two young doctors, one inside industry, the other in public health. Both were young, fresh out of school, and coming of professional age in an era of social activism. Both saw it as their responsibility to help those who were ill and—as with Bouhuys—to find out what it was about their work that was making them so. Not dramatic notions perhaps, but ones we have seen too rarely in the story of byssinosis so far.

The tangled tale of Schrag's paper illustrates the battles that go on at the juncture of public health science and industrial self-interest, and the hobbled way in which science must operate when its laboratory is, in effect, someone else's floor. It also shows how even the best in public health science may take this hobbling as a given, reify it, defend and reinforce it in the name of "proper channels," "professional responsibility," and "scientific integrity."

As it turned out, the story did not end with the publication of Schrag's and Gullett's study in the *American Review of Respiratory Disease* [6]. Schrag did take his knowledge of byssinosis to Ralph Nader, and Nader, who had strongly supported the Black Lung struggle of coal miners, was interested. Nader has reflected that his interest may in part have been due to memories of growing up in Winstead, Connecticut, a cotton textile town, and of seeing mill workers covered in lint grabbing hurried meals at his father's restaurant [7].

Nader learned of Bouhuys' difficulties with the Georgia textile industry, the state of knowledge about byssinosis in the United States, the danger facing many textile workers. In 1971, he would publish in *The Nation* an article called "Brown Lung: The Cotton Mill Killer" [8]. The piece would do much to bring public attention to the all but unknown disease.

As the 1970s began, then, the secret was out. Byssinosis would no longer be "mysterious"; it would become, for a time a least, a topic of national concern, of national shame, of national struggle.

ENDNOTES

1. W. J. Cash, *The Mind of the South,* Doubleday Anchor, Garden City, 1954.
2. The cited biographical information is contained in a correspondence from Schrag to Charles Levenstein, 3/20/83.
3. Interview with Gullett conducted by Ira Burnim, June 1983.
4. Exactly why Fieldcrest hired Gullett is a matter of speculation. He did, as noted, enjoy strong support from at least one executive, and perhaps Fieldcrest was genuinely concerned over the question of byssinosis. It was also perhaps, given the changing tenor of the times, a good public relations move. Or, perhaps Fieldcrest was simply indifferent to Gullett's interest in byssinosis.
5. Schrag to Newton, 3/19/68. This correspondence and all others hereafter cited in this chapter have been provided by Peter Shuck of New Haven, Connecticut.

6. Peter Schrag and A. Dale Gullett, Byssinosis in Cotton Mills, *American Review of Respiratory Disease*, 101, 1970.
7. Interview with Nader conducted by Charles Levenstein, June 1983.
8. Ralph Nader, Brown Lung: The Cotton Mill Killer, *The Nation, 212,* pp. 335-337, March 15, 1971. Nader is generally credited with coining the term "brown lung."

CHAPTER 10

Full Circle: "Burlington's Disease"

VENAL DOCTORS AND INFERIOR RACES

The textile industry had an image problem. By the late 1960s, Southern mill owners were being buffeted by social, political, and economic forces over which they could no longer exercise the paternalistic control they had long been accustomed to. The Civil Rights Movement had bared to the nation the oppressive hierarchy and racism that lay just beneath the genteel pretensions of the "Southern way of life." The Movement was also, to be fair, showing that conditions for African Americans in the North were not much better, if better at all.

In the wake of the Civil Rights Movement, other progressive and grass roots initiatives had also emerged. Best known, of course, were the student and anti-war movements, but workers were rebelling as well, and among the sources of their discontent were the health and safety conditions under which they labored, issues more often than not ignored by national union officials [1]. The number of "wildcat strikes," work stoppages in violation of "no strike" agreements in union contracts and usually against the wishes of top union leaderships, rose dramatically between 1967 and 1969. While these spontaneous actions did not often result in permanent organizations, they did indicate a high level of worker discontent with the immediate conditions of the workplace and also with their own unions.

One grass roots movement that did affect significant change, however, was the 1969 protests of coal miners in West Virginia and Kentucky over conditions in the mines. Consolidating their efforts through the formation of the Black Lung Association, the miners were able to engage in significant action that showed their ability to seriously disrupt the industry. In West Virginia, for example, 43,000 miners—against the wishes of their own union, the United Mine Workers— succeeded in shutting down the mines for three weeks. Faced with such labor militancy and solidarity, the U.S. Congress passed the Coal Mine Safety and

Health Act which addressed many of the concerns of the Black Lung Association. Beyond this immediate gain, the formation and activities of the Association played a significant role in placing workplace health and safety issues onto the public policy agenda and also into the consciousness of the American public.

Still, due to its traditional weakness, labor in the United States is seldom in a position to unilaterally win demands whether in government or in public opinion. In the late 1960s, though, other groups were showing an increasing awareness of and interest in issues of workplace health and safety. A middle-class environmental movement was emerging and was uncovering the extent of corporate indifference to the environmental damage its production activities had engendered. Ralph Nader had brought to public attention the irresponsibility and unaccountability of corporate action. In 1969, a team of "Nader's raiders" had, for instance, revealed what they found to be the lax enforcement of health and safety regulations within the Departments of Labor and Health, Education, and Welfare.

Thus, a commonality of interests allowed insurgent labor to work with leaders of environmental groups and consumer interest groups to form an effective lobby for federal regulation of the workplace. They were joined by progressives and activists among occupational health professionals, key labor activists such as Anthony Mazzochi of the Oil, Chemical, and Atomic Workers union, and eventually certain major unions such as the United Steel Workers of America. Also, the issue of occupational health and safety enjoyed a generally favorable press.

This coalition was, in turn, dealing with an administration that was highly receptive to the idea of such federal regulation. Wishing to carry on the Great Society, but wary of spending yet more federal dollars, the Johnson administration saw the federal regulation of workplace health and safety as both a popular and cheap answer to their problem. Such regulation would placate the Democrats' allies in labor but at the same time could be presented as a "quality of life" issue and not simply a political gift to a "special interest." Finally, industry itself would pay much of the cost through compliance with such regulation. Thus, in January 1968 Johnson proposed the Occupational Safety and Health Act. It would become law in 1970, creating the Occupational Safety and Health Administration (OSHA) which was given broad responsibility for health and safety standard setting and enforcement. While OSHA has delivered far less than it promised, its significance in the struggle for a safer workplace should not be dismissed [2].

How did this new national concern with occupational health and safety affect the South and the textile industry? In one sense it had very little effect, in another sense it mattered a great deal. There is little evidence, for instance, of a significant increase in labor unrest or labor organizing in the mills during the late 1960s, although in the mid-1970s the Brown Lung Association would be formed to struggle for just compensation for victims of byssinosis and the Amalgamated Clothing and Textile Workers Union would step up its organizing activities. But on the whole, labor pressure on Southern textiles seems to have been more indirect.

No doubt national attention to health and safety on the job made some mill workers less fatalistic about the issue, though they did not need a national campaign to tell them about conditions in the mills. Economic changes, though, were having a greater impact. Overall, unemployment was low in the South and the Southern economy was beginning to diversify as the great industrial migration to the South was underway. Many workers, then, had other options than laboring in the dirty, dangerous, and exhausting textile mills for very low pay. Attracting workers to the mills was becoming a problem.

The same was true for white collar employees such as engineers and managers. The mills simply were not attractive places to work. Beardsley explains:

> In a decade which saw most of the nation agonize over problems of poverty, discrimination, and injustice, textiles were seen as an industry which did not care about people and which came down on the wrong side of every issue. And that image hurt, not least in the recruiting area, as the industry sought to attract bright young engineers and business graduates [3, p. 239].

Finally, if the negative image of the mills was hurting the recruiting of line workers and high quality technical and managerial personnel, it surely must have been a concern that this image would also hurt sales.

So while Southern textiles were not necessarily facing the direct pressure to improve health and safety other industries such as coal were, their poor record in this area was having economic consequences. The image problem of the textile industry, as *Textile World* editor L. A. Christiansen wrote at the time, "affects almost every aspect of . . . business" [quoted in 3, p. 239].

Then there was byssinosis. The issue would not go away. In the past, investigations or studies that indicated a problem with byssinosis in the mills could be quietly filed and forgotten. Such was the fate in the United States of the work of British investigators, of Trice, of the Harvard Cotton Dust Project, of Liberty Mutual, of Dickson, McLean, and others. But by the late 1960s, too much evidence was accumulating, too many people were interested.

While hardly rebels in any conventional sense, Schrag and Bouhuys, in particular, had shown themselves willing to challenge both the power of the mills and the accepted procedures and etiquette of occupational health and safety professionals, at the risk of their careers. In this, they both reflected their times, and contributed to them.

Nor were state health departments as willing as in the past to bow to pressures to tread lightly as far as the textile industry was concerned. The industry itself, though still a force, did not have quite the power it once had to cajole state legislatures into reining in these departments. And there was little doubt that if OSHA came into being the textile industry would be one of its targets.

In the face of all these challenges, the mill owners, on the whole, continued to pursue their age old strategy we have described earlier in this book, quoting Beardsley:

> From the start the strategy of Southern mill owners when accused of harboring serious health hazards in their factories was either to ignore the charges, deflect them, or defame those who raised them.

In the 1950s and into the 1960s, as we have seen, Ted M. Forbes and the Georgia Textile Manufacturing Association raised this strategy of deflection and denial to an art form. In the later 1960s, not much had changed among the mill owners. Though some smaller mills, such as Fieldcrest, did allow studies to take place in their premises—if not publication of these studies—and did institute medical surveillance of their workers, the industry on the whole continued to challenge the connection between cotton dust and byssinosis and to resist government intervention in their workplaces.

The textile industry, as with many other industries, remained adamantly opposed to the OSH Act. After the Act passed and OSHA was created, the industry fought to prevent the new agency from issuing a standard for permissible levels of exposure to cotton dust. When that standard was proposed in late 1976, textile owners sued to prevent its implementation. The suit was finally decided by the Supreme Court—the mill owners lost—but not until 1981. During the Reagan administration, mill owners worked to weaken the standards OSHA had set.

So, to say the least, the textile industry did not go gentle into that good night of federal regulation. In 1969, though not every mill owner necessarily agreed wholeheartedly with it, the industry could not have made its position clearer. This from an unsigned editorial in the industry journal *American Textile Reporter* (July 1969):

> We are particularly intrigued by the term "Byssinosis," a thing thought up by venal doctors who attended last year's ILO meeting in Africa where inferior races are bound to be afflicted by new disease more superior people defeated years ago. . . . Well, we would want to tell Mr. O'Hara [Michigan Representative who co-sponsored the Occupational Health and Safety bill in Congress], and for all of our life, we have hated federal intervention in our lives and businesses. . . . Congressman O'Hara is typical of the lousy representation we get from time-serving Northern Democrats who sell their souls to the venal labor leaders [quoted in 4, p. 122; also quoted in 3, p. 239].

Although under pressure in the late 1960s, then, the textile industry remained defiant and recalcitrant, and it retained two powerful weapons in the face of its enemies—the first was political, the second scientific. Politically, the industry was able to maintain the united front it had always held against the imprecations of "outsiders." One only need recall how quickly Forbes and the GTMA reacted when a few owners were considering allowing studies in their mills by state health officials (see Chapter 7). Scientifically, while the studies of Bouhuys and others strongly suggested that the etiology of byssinosis lay in the breathing of cotton dust, no large scale epidemiological study had ever been done, or more accurately had ever been allowed to be done, in U.S. mills. Stronger scientific evidence was lacking and the united front insured things would stay that way.

In 1969, however, one member of the industry defected. Its action both broke down the united front and provided compelling evidence that byssinosis was indeed a disease of the cotton mills. In that year, Burlington Industries allowed an epidemiological study of 10,133 of its mill employees, 95 percent of the total. How and why Burlington Industries took this action and its repercussions are the topics we explore in the rest of this chapter.

THE STUDY AND ITS ORIGINS

Calvin Michaels had done well at Burlington Industries [5]. In 1968, after service as personnel director at one of Burlington's many divisions, he had been appointed to the top corporate staff as Vice-President of Personnel. The newly christened "Department of Personnel Administration" he headed was growing in size and importance within Burlington, and Michaels had the opportunity to do well for the company, as well as for himself.

It was about this time, Michaels recalls, that he became aware of the dispute going on between Peter Schrag and Fieldcrest Mills over Schrag's insistence that he be allowed to publish his study of byssinosis. Michaels was also interested in, as well he should have been, the political whirlwind surrounding the proposed creation of OSHA and the strong possibility that some sort of federal regulation and inspection of the textile industry might soon be a reality. How prepared was Burlington to deal with the demands OSHA was likely to make on them?

At the time, Burlington had a strong safety program but, as with most textile firms, not much of a health program. Burlington had grown, in part, by buying up smaller companies. If the purchased company had a nurse on its staff, Burlington would keep her on, but she would not be part of any large or coordinated occupational health initiative within the corporation, because there was none. Burlington would also, of course, inherit whatever health and safety problems might exist in a purchased company [6].

Michaels also became aware at this time that no one on the corporate staff knew much of anything about byssinosis or the growing controversy surrounding it. While this may be overstating the case—it seems highly unlikely that at this late date everyone at Burlington was ignorant of the disease—the top management of Burlington appeared to be generally interested in learning more about the disease and also in creating within the corporation an occupational health or medical program [7]. Once this corporate mandate was in place, events started happening quickly.

As Michaels was beginning his new position at Burlington, Dr. James Merchant arrived at the North Carolina Department of Health. At the time an officer of the Epidemiological Intelligence Service (EIS), Merchant was replacing Peter Schrag as an epidemiologist in the Health Department's Epidemiology Division.

Merchant had first become interested in byssinosis while attending an EIS program at which Schrag had discussed his Fieldcrest study. In North Carolina he began working with the industrial hygienist John Lumsden in a search for possible research opportunities on the disease [8].

They contacted Dr. Ben Drake, local county health director in Gastonia, who in turn put them in touch with mill owner A. M. Smyre who allowed them—according to Merchant, due to a paternalistic concern for his workers—to do an epidemiological study of his plant. Merchant and Lumsden found that 20 percent of the workers in the card room showed signs of byssinosis.

Shortly thereafter, a weaver at a Burlington mill in Gastonia contacted Dr. Drake and complained of byssinosis-like symptoms. Drake referred the complaint to Merchant and Lumsden. They were allowed a walk through the plant by the mill manager, but he refused to let them do a study. On the advice of his boss, Dr. Martin Hines—who had a brother working in the mills and knew mill owner mentality—Merchant kept sending information to the mill manager, such material as the results of British investigations and the results of his and Lumsden's own work at the Smyre plant. Dr. Merchant has estimated that he wrote three or more letters over a six-month period [8].

Merchant's persistence apparently paid off, as Michaels remembers becoming aware of the complaint lodged by the worker in Burlington's Gastonia plant. It is probable the mill manager also forwarded the information Merchant had provided.

Though the exact sequence of events during these months is confusing, apparently Michaels did not immediately contact Merchant and Lumsden but first turned to Burlington's workers' compensation insurance carrier, Liberty Mutual.

Liberty Mutual did a quick analysis and found that workers at the Gastonia plant were reacting to bacteria growing in sediment that built up over the weekend in the plant's humidifiers. This was not, then, a case of byssinosis, but the incident does seem to have been the beginning of Burlington's attempt to learn what it could about the disease from Liberty Mutual.

A group from Burlington then traveled to Liberty Mutual's home office, but received no more than "fragmented literature" about byssinosis and some information about the work Bouhuys was doing. Liberty Mutual simply didn't know much about byssinosis. This was true enough. Although Liberty Mutual was certainly aware of byssinosis at the time and even earlier, its general approach—as we have discussed in Chapter 6—seems to have been to avoid the issue. In short, then, Liberty Mutual couldn't tell Burlington if it had a byssinosis problem or if it didn't [9].

Burlington wished to pursue a study of byssinosis in its plants, but managers were left asking the question "how do you do it." According to Michaels, they went looking for university help. Michaels turned to Dr. Mario Battigelli of Duke University Medical School who they believed had expertise in the area. Battigelli thought there might indeed be a problem but knew of no research teams ready to investigate the problem. Michaels and Battigelli then met with Burlington Vice-President Charles McClendon who showed enthusiasm for the project.

With this green light, the two then prepared a team of researchers, turning first to Kaye Kilburn who was at the time the Director of the Division of Environmental Medicine at Duke; prior to that he had been Chief of Medical Services at the VA hospital connected with Duke [10]. It was while serving in this earlier position that Kilburn had corresponded with and provided important records on VA patients to Bouhuys (see Chapter 8). Kilburn had knowledge of byssinosis and also had a number of advanced students who could be put to work on the project. He eventually agreed, after some persuasion, to oversee the investigation.

One question that came up at this time, again according to Michaels, was that of funding. Burlington was concerned that if it alone funded the study it would raise issues of credibility, so it was then that the decision was made to turn to the North Carolina Department of Health. Michaels and McClendon met with Merchant and Lumsden to inquire into their interest in doing epidemiological work at Burlington [8]. After this, a number of other persons also joined the research, from Duke, from the state Health Department, and from Burlington Industries itself.

Michaels had put together within the Department of Personnel Administration an impressive group of occupational health and safety professionals— epidemiologists, industrial hygienists, physicians, biostatisticians, engineers. Merchant was responsible for identifying the plants that would be used in the initial study. Merchant and Kilburn agreed that the dirtiest among the plants, the plant with the most severe cotton dust problem, was located in Smithfield. After preliminary epidemiological investigation there, Kilburn presided over a symposium held at Duke University.

The purpose of the symposium was to discuss what was generally known about byssinosis, and also what had been learned so far about the problem at Burlington. Kilburn noted that, although not all workers seemed affected, there was indeed a problem at Smithfield and more studies should be done. Merchant estimated that overall, throughout the industry, 25 percent of workers exposed to cotton dust could develop byssinosis [11]. The consensus was that expanded epidemiological studies should proceed, and Burlington agreed [12].

Perhaps what is most intriguing about this symposium is that, although it was presented as a purely academic conference, Burlington footed the bill. It did so, however, indirectly; Burlington "donated" a large sum of money to Duke, and Duke in turn used this money to fund the conference [6]. Clearly, Burlington did not yet want its heavy involvement in investigating byssinosis to become known to the rest of the industry.

Merchant and his colleagues were ready to proceed with their five-plant study, but another problem remained. At the time, there was no effective method for accurately measuring the amount of cotton dust in the air, of separating respirable dust from the total amount of dust in the air. In the past, studies had sometimes shown that the dustiest area of a plant had the lowest byssinosis rate [8].

Burlington found that neither Liberty Mutual nor equipment manufacturers for the industry had a device for such measurement in development and so Burlington's own Research and Development Department went to work. They helped develop what is called a "vertical elutriator," and it worked. Or, in the more precise scientific terms of Merchant,

> The vertical elutriator cotton dust sampler . . . has proven to be a durable and practical instrument which collects a biologically active lint free fraction of dust linearly associated with indicators of biological response [13].

If by 1970 byssinosis headed the list of health and safety issues among Burlington's top management, there were other concerns as well, including excessive noise and hearing reduction, chemical hazards such as formaldehyde that was used in the production of perma press fabric, and general safety problems. Management at this time, as Michaels notes, "needed to gear up for the new OSHA law," so it desired to have these problems examined but also wished to create an ongoing and coordinated health and safety program that would engage in research, medical surveillance of workers, routine clinical duties, as well as worker education [6, Imbus lecture, Venable interview].

To this end, in February 1970 Michaels hired Dr. Harold R. Imbus, who previously had worked at the Kennedy Space Center, as Burlington's first Medical Director. Imbus seems to have been an energetic and capable administrator and in short order became responsible for all of Burlington's health and safety efforts, thus moving these efforts out of Personnel Administration and the direct supervision of Michaels, although Imbus was to continue to report to Michaels, who in turn reported to McClendon, who reported to the Board of Directors [6, Imbus lecture].

Imbus also acquired a corporate staff of 21 people, including two physicians, a Director of Nursing (Ann Murphy), a top safety engineer (Charles Crocker), and the industrial hygienist John Neehas [14]. In 1970, 25 nurses were also hired, and by 1972 there were over 100 nurses on the Burlington payroll. Initially, their primary duty was to carry out respiratory surveillance of mill workers but their work soon expanded into other areas [6, Imbus lecture, Venable interview].

And, of course, Imbus became deeply involved in the ongoing byssinosis investigations. By around the end of 1970, Merchant's epidemiological study of five plants was complete. The results were shocking—though they probably should not have been, given what was already known about byssinosis—and Merchant's prediction turned out to be a conservative one: approximately 38 percent of workers evaluated, at a specific level of cotton dust exposure, showed byssinotic symptoms, and the problem was most severe in the card room where cotton dust levels were highest. In his study, however, Merchant concluded that,

> . . . it appears that there is no work area in the cotton mills that could be considered reasonably or marginally safe, although yarn processing and weaving areas are not far from these levels.

He also noted that,

> . . . there appears to be no threshold beneath which no one with Monday chest tightness (a symptom of the early stage of byssinosis) was found. This indication that low dust concentrations result in measurable effects suggests that cotton dust is a highly biologically active inhalant [15, pp. 28-29].

Burlington had a problem, and by extension so did the cotton textile industry. But rather than attempt to suppress or deny Merchant's findings, as would likely have occurred in the past, these findings were the catalyst for a much larger study. Imbus became the lead investigator of an epidemiological survey of *all* of Burlington's mills. When the results of this study were in, in 1971, they did not differ appreciably from those of Merchant (even if the numbers were somewhat lower and presented in a less dramatic and more circumspect fashion). As Imbus has said, "Card room for card room (there were) similar findings." Although Imbus emphasized that overall throughout Burlington's cotton mills the rate for byssinosis was 5.2 percent, the overall rate in the card room area was 26.2 percent [16].

The importance of these two studies cannot be overemphasized. Although earlier work, especially that of Bouhuys, had gone far in suggesting the etiology of byssinosis and indicating its presence in the cotton mills, no similarly extensive epidemiological studies had ever been undertaken in the United States, and without the cooperation and involvement of Burlington they never would have happened. Burlington did much to conceal this involvement, but was not entirely successful. Michaels reports that industry organizations were quite upset with what Burlington was up to. They would get more upset. Both Merchant's study and that of Imbus openly acknowledged the support of Burlington and that their work had taken place in Burlington mills.

Most significantly, after the results of the Imbus study were made public Vice-President Charles McClendon publicly announced:

> Byssinosis can be clinically diagnosed and is attributable to cotton dust [quoted in 3, p. 241].

Many years of struggle over byssinosis were to follow (and continue today)—over its exact etiology, over questions of compensation, over PELs (Permissible Exposure Limits to cotton dust), and other issues. But McClendon's words were a turning point. The largest and most powerful firm in the textile industry had broken ranks and publicly admitted what many mill owners had already known or suspected for decade after decade: byssinosis is an occupational disease. For some time after the work of Imbus and Merchant became known, byssinosis was also called "Burlington's Disease," reflecting both the tremendous influence of these investigations and the sense of betrayal they had engendered among others in the textile industry [6, Imbus lecture]. Deflection and denial among the mill owners would never, could never, work quite as well again.

THINGS ARE NOT ALWAYS WHAT THEY APPEAR

Despite the collaborative nature of their work at Burlington, tensions soon appeared among the researchers at Burlington. The odd man out seems to have been Merchant. Michaels comments that Merchant never understood how "traumatic" the results of the byssinosis surveys had been for Burlington, and that over time he took on an "independence" not previously evident. Finally, Michaels suggests Merchant "overstated" how serious the problem was in the mills. Though Michaels put his own spin on it, it does seem true that Merchant did view byssinosis as a more serious problem in the mills than did some of the other researchers at Burlington.

The issues that divided Merchant and other researchers at Burlington are many and often arcane and complex. We will mention only two.

As early as their initial studies, Merchant and Imbus seemed to have differed over how great an emphasis to put on engineering and environmental controls versus medical surveillance. In his study, Merchant lists specific engineering changes that should be made to limit the amount of cotton dust being breathed by mill workers, and concludes with the following:

> . . . a successful occupational health program for the cotton dust industry should include efforts to remove or reduce cotton dust prior to processing, efficient machine exhaust and ventilation systems, and medical surveillance . . . [15, p. 230].

Imbus acknowledges environmental controls are vital but is less specific in his recommendations and concludes by saying,

> . . . it is generally agreed that any currently proposed methods of environmental control will not be completely effective. Therefore, the need for medical surveillance will probably continue for some time [16, p. 191].[1]

The differences here are subtle and ones of emphasis, but nonetheless real. They represent, no doubt, the differences in perspective between a public health investigator and a corporate representative and employee.

A more important disagreement between the two concerned cigarette smoking. Both Merchant and Imbus concurred in the finding that, as Merchant put it in his study, "smokers had a significantly higher prevalence of byssinosis" [15, p. 230]. But how much of the breathing problems of mill workers was attributable

---

[1] As we discuss below, Burlington did later develop and implement technology that significantly reduced cotton dust in the card room.

to smoking and how much to byssinosis contracted through the inhalation of cotton dust? Over the years, Imbus would tend to reflect the position of the American Textile Manufacturers Institute that smoking was perhaps a more important variable than cotton dust in explaining such problems [17].

Merchant of course warned of the dangers of smoking, but nevertheless insisted that cotton dust in and of itself clearly was responsible for the contraction of byssinosis. In comments before the House Committee on Education and Labor Subcommittee on Labor Standards (May 15, 1980), Merchant noted that,

> Many cross-sectional epidemiological studies show significantly more airways obstruction among exposed workers than controls, even after accounting for smoking, age, and other risk factors.

He added,

> Prospective studies of cotton textile workers reveal a two to tenfold annual decrease in lung function, as compared with unexposed populations. Smoking alone has been found to result in a twofold annual decrease in lung function.

The differences between Merchant and Imbus reflect the broader differences among health care professionals. Merchant, Bouhuys, and others continued to insist on the knowable if complex etiology of byssinosis as an occupational disease and stalwartly defended the right of mill workers to be compensated for that disease. Imbus, Battigelli, and others generally reflected the industry's continuing challenges, as we have noted, to the etiology of byssinosis, to the level of proof needed for compensation, to the cotton dust standard proposed by OSHA, and even to the right of OSHA to propose the standard at all. That they did so is not surprising—they worked for the industry. (Though this is in no way meant to besmirch their scientific integrity.) The surprising fact is this: Dr. Harold R. Imbus, Medical Director for Burlington Industries, wrote the OSHA cotton dust standard.

Shortly after the completion of the Burlington studies, Imbus received a telephone call from Grover Wren who at the time was head of the OSHA standards office. As really the only large epidemiological studies of byssinosis in the cotton mills, and as they indicated a serious problem, the Burlington studies had been an influencing factor in OSHA's decision to regulate the cotton textile industry through the issuance of a standard. Wren asked Imbus if he would be willing to write a draft for this standard. Imbus agreed. Although not involved in actually deciding the PEL for cotton dust, he did create the general format for the document and much of the substantive information the standard would contain—on requirements, for instance, for recordkeeping, medical surveillance, air sampling, engineering controls [6, Imbus lecture. See also OSHA Standard Number 1910.1043].

Burlington seems not to have had a problem with Imbus working with OSHA; in fact they gave him time off to do so. What Burlington did try to do, however, was keep this information from the rest of the industry [6, Imbus lecture]. Most of the other mill owners, to say the least, were upset with Burlington over its studies and its public statements concerning them. If they learned what Imbus was up to—as of course they eventually did—their reaction would be predictable.

Throughout its history, the cotton textile industry had shown in word and deed that it ". . . hated federal intervention in our lives and businesses." In 1976, their worst nightmare came true when OSHA issued its initial proposal for a cotton dust standard. A federal agency now had unprecedented power to regulate, investigate, and fine the industry. And, one of their own had lent a hand in defining and creating this unwanted intrusion that had invaded their lives.

WHY BURLINGTON?

Why did Burlington allow the Merchant and Imbus studies to take place in its mills? Why did it publicly admit cotton dust caused byssinosis? Why did it allow its Medical Director to work with OSHA to create a cotton dust standard?

One answer is, these were the right things to do. According to John Lumsden, when Merchant and he were approached by Michaels and Charles McClendon about doing an epidemiological survey at Burlington, McClendon's words were, "If there is something wrong, we want to know about it" [18]. Michaels recalls that he "never had trouble in convincing management to do something for employees" [6, Michaels interview]. Merchant found Burlington very helpful and that its attitude departed from the "stonewalling" mentality of most of the rest of the industry [8]. Imbus has simply said that Burlington had "progressive management" [6, Imbus lecture].

We need not doubt Burlington's altruistic concern for its workers, to ask if there weren't other things going on. This is, after all, something of a selective altruism in two ways. First, it seems not to have been the general attitude of the industry; second, if Burlington had acted solely out of concern for its workers, it seems reasonable that at least someone in management as late as 1968-69 would have known something about byssinosis, would at least have heard of it, might have acted earlier to find out if something was wrong. But, according to Michaels, no one did.

Burlington's acquiescence to studies in its mills coincides with a time of a growing image problem for the cotton textile industry, as we have discussed above. Burlington was not immune to the negative consequences of this problem in terms of recruiting workers and technical personnel, in terms of sales. Workplace health and safety was on the national agenda anyway, and pressure on the textile industry over byssinosis was on the rise. So it made sense for Burlington to choose cooperation over confrontation; this would enhance its own image and also distinguish it from other, more recalcitrant competitors in the industry such as J. P. Stevens which had been the object of protest over its employment policies since the late 1950s and would soon face a national boycott [19]. Altruism and image enhancement could go hand in hand [20].

But why didn't these strategies make business sense to more mill owners? The answer seems to be, they made business sense if you could afford it, and Burlington could.

Burlington was by far the largest firm in the cotton textile industry and one of the most technologically advanced. In 1968, net sales for Burlington were approximately $1.6 billion, in 1969 $1.7 billion, in 1970 $1.8 billion. The figures for J. P. Stevens are as follows: 1968—$963 million, 1969—$1 billion, 1970—$893 million. After Burlington and J. P. Stevens, net sales figures drop dramatically, the average for the top 12 companies in 1969, for instance, was $512 million (see Table 1). So, during these years, J. P. Stevens was fairly competitive with Burlington, but no other firm was even close.

Burlington also comes out on top when figures for changes in their net fixed assets as percent of invested capital, a reasonable indicator of technological innovation, are looked at. In 1965, Burlington's net fixed assets were valued at $314.6 million, 42.6 percent of invested capital. In 1970, the numbers were $625.2 million and 54 percent. For J. P. Stevens in 1965, net fixed assets were valued at $161.4 million, 36.1 percent of investment capital; 1970: $194.6 million, 37 percent. Other top companies had larger percentage changes between these two dates, but none approaches the real value of Burlington's net fixed assets (see Table 2).

Burlington, then, dominated the industry and it could continue to do so by improving efficiency through investment in technology. Plus, it would not

Table 1. Net Sales, 12 Top Textile Companies, 1965-1970
(millions of dollars)

Company	1965	1966	1967	1968	1969	1970
Burlington	1313	1372	1365	1619	1765	1822
Stevens	805	855	846	963	1003	893
United Merchants	560	601	607	652	695	708
Lowenstein	289	301	291	338	377	387
WestPoint-Pepperell	317	352	335	347	372	374
Springs	249	249	243	253	293	308
Cannon	N/A	291	287	308	299	306
Mohasco	296	265	261	295	312	306
Cone	254	284	263	262	279	298
Dan River	257	292	266	295	300	293
Collins & Aikman	168	178	186	215	223	240
Kendall	174	181	191	210	231	238

Source: TW '71-'72 fact file, p. 23, July 1971.

Table 2. Net Fixed Assets as Percent of Invested Capital, 1965-1970
(assets in millions of dollars)

Company	1965		1970	
	Assets	Percent	Assets	Percent
Burlington	314.6	42.6	625.2	54.0
Stevens	161.4	36.1	194.6	37.0
United Merchants	75.6	32.0	123.2	29.8
Lowenstein	54.6	33.9	99.2	56.0
WestPoint-Pepperell	57.5	35.9	89.6	47.4
Springs	122.8	48.9	179.0	63.0
Cannon	55.5	30.3	88.6	40.0
Mohasco	65.8	52.5	80.8	44.0
Cone	67.9	44.5	74.8	46.0
Dan River	84.3	49.8	96.4	46.0
Collins & Aikman	N/A	N/A	66.3	59.0
Kendall	35.5	38.1	72.3	53.7

Source: TW '71-'72 fact file, p. 23, July 1971.

necessarily cost Burlington nearly as much to clean up its mills as it would less profitable, less technologically advanced firms. More modernized facilities tended to be cleaner anyway, so Burlington might even profit from the recognition of byssinosis and the imposition by OSHA of a cotton dust standard [21]. Also, though this was not necessarily their purpose, in attempting to meet cotton dust standards, lesser firms might lose profits or simply go out of business, which did occur as foreign competition began to hit the industry hard in the later 1970s and 1980s. Acknowledging that cotton dust caused byssinosis, then, simply made good business sense in the case of Burlington.

CONCLUSION

The case of Burlington Industries and byssinosis brings us full circle.

As we discussed in Chapter 2, in 1911 the suck shuttle was banned in Massachusetts textile mills due to a convergence of historical forces—a strong labor movement with political influence, public health officials and other health care professionals with a desire to enact the ban, a general public that was conscious of and concerned over TB, a responsive state government, a favorable press, a divided industry. Opposition to the ban tended to be stronger among mills that were relatively less technologically advanced, and support tended to be stronger among more advanced mills—for instance, the Fall River Iron Works—and among manufacturers of new, automatic loom machinery—for instance, the

Draper Corporation. While the ban was never completely successful, it was one of the earliest examples of attempts to regulate occupational disease in the United States by intervening in the production process.

The interaction among these various forces, or actors, is complex and it cannot be said that any single one was decisive in the banning of the suck shuttle. Rather, an historical moment was created in which the possibility of state action in the name of protecting occupational health became extant. Further, had any of these forces been missing, or acted differently than it did, the ban most likely would not have occurred, although proving a negative is of course difficult. In any event, it would be another 60 years or so before another convergence of historical forces would lead to government intervention in the productive processes of the textile industry.

In the late 1960s, as we have seen, dissident labor, consumer and environmental groups, progressive occupational health professionals, labor activists, and certain union leaders were putting strong pressure on the federal government to more aggressively address problems of health and safety in the workplace. Also, consciousness of such problems was growing among the general population and the press was generally sympathetic to those groups working to improve the situation.

Facing this pressure, and for its own reasons, the federal government responded by proposing the OSH Act and the creation of OSHA, an organization that would enjoy strong, if limited, power to regulate the work practices of U.S. industry. In the early- and middle-1970s activists and the press would turn their attention to the textile industry, and in 1976 OSHA would propose a cotton dust standard. In the meantime the textile industry was facing mounting pressure from occupational health professionals in government and academia to allow more studies of their mills, especially in connection with the problem of byssinosis.

While much of the cotton textile industry responded through deflection and denial, Burlington Industries broke ranks, allowed epidemiological studies to take place in their mills, publicly admitted cotton dust caused byssinosis, and played a central role in the writing of the cotton dust standard.

By the early 1970s, then, byssinosis had at last become recognized as an occupational disease and thus compensable. Though this victory was far from total—debates over the etiology of byssinosis, PELs, compensation continue to this day—this recognition was an important breakthrough.

As in the case of the suck shuttle, an historical moment had been created in which the possibility of state action in the name of protecting occupational health became extant. The interaction of the various forces that brought this moment into being, again as with the suck shuttle ban, is complex and no single force was decisive in the recognition of byssinosis. Had any of these forces been missing or acted differently, the recognition of byssinosis might not have occurred, or occurred so soon or so forcefully.

Had there not been strong activism, public concern, and government pressure, why would Burlington have opened up its mills? It had not done so in the past. Yet if Burlington had not opened up the mills, the presence of byssinosis in the cotton industry would have been less of a scientific certainty and the pressure on the rest of the industry to take steps to limit the amount of cotton dust in their workplaces would in all likelihood not have been as great. Finally, it took the willingness of the federal government to use the scientific evidence that led to the cotton dust standard.

In our concluding chapter, we turn to a fuller examination of the theoretical and practical implications of our examination of "The Cotton Dust Papers."

ENDNOTES

1. The following discussion on coalition building around occupational health and safety issues draws on Charles Noble, *Liberalism at Work,* Temple University Press, Philadelphia, pp. 70-89, 1986.
2. One indication of the broad national concern at this time for health and safety in the workplace was the wide popularity of a series of articles by Paul Brodeur that appeared in the *New Yorker* in the early 1970s. In this award winning series, Brodeur presented a—highly accurate—portrait of how industrial and governmental indifference and malfeasance had led to a virtual epidemic of disease and death among workers due to the unregulated or under-regulated presence of hazardous chemicals and substances in the workplace. This series later was compiled into the book *Expendable Americans,* The Viking Press, New York, 1973.
3. Edward H. Beardsley, *A History of Neglect: Health Care for Blacks and Mill Workers in the Twentieth-Century South,* University of Tennessee, Knoxville, 1987.
4. Robert E. Botsch, *Organizing the Breathless: Cotton Dust, Southern Politics, and the Brown Lung Association,* The University Press of Kentucky, Lexington, 1993.
5. A good deal of what we discuss in this section is based on an extensive interview with Calvin Michaels conducted by Charles Levenstein, 3/18/83.
6. Michaels interview. Harold Imbus, Medical Director for Burlington from 1970 to 1981, and Carol Venable, Assistant Director of Nursing at Burlington in the 1970s, later Coordinator of Nurses Education and Health Education, and an early participant in the creation of a medical department within Burlington, make similar points about the lack of any health or medical program at Burlington at the time. Imbus: public lecture, notes, Harvard University, 12/16/81. Venable: interview with Charles Levenstein, 3/18/83.
7. It will be recalled from Chapter 6 that in 1966 the ACGIH had set a cotton dust standard of 1 mg per cubic meter. In 1968 the Department of Labor adopted this standard within the Walsh-Healey Act, whose rules applied to all companies doing business with the government. See [4, p. 192]. It is likely Burlington was aware of this standard, or that at least its workers' compensation carrier, Liberty Mutual, was.
8. Phone interview with Dr. James Merchant conducted by Gregory F. DeLaurier, 6/20/00.
9. According to Michaels, the failure of Liberty Mutual to provide adequate "service" to Burlington, in terms of providing research on and information about health and safety risks, caused the corporation to later drop Liberty Mutual as its workers'

compensation carrier and become self-insured. See also interview with Donald Hayes, Director of Health and Safety for Burlington during the 1980s, conducted by Charles Levenstein, 3/18/83.

10. Kaye H. Kilburn, curriculum vitae, http://www.neuro-test.com/Khk_cv.htm.

11. Merchant's comment is noted by Botsch in [4, p. 192].

12. See, The Status of Byssinosis in the United States: A Summary of the National Conference on Cotton Dust and Health and the Recommendation of the Organizing Committee, *Archive of Environmental Health, 23*, pp. 230-234, 1971.

13. James A. Merchant et al., Dose Response Studies in Cotton Textile Workers, *Journal of Medicine, 15*:3, pp. 220-230, March 1973. Merchant recalls that Lumsden and two other industrial hygienists, Howard Ayre and Jerry Lynch, literally drew the design for the elutriator on a napkin in a diner in Smithfield. Merchant interview.

14. Interview with Charles Crocker conducted by Charles Levenstein, 3/18/83.

15. James A. Merchant et al., Dose Response Studies in Cotton Textile Workers, *Journal of Medicine,* 1973.

16. Harold Imbus and Moon W. Suh, Byssinosis: A Study of 10,133 Textile Workers, *Archive of Environmental Health, 26,* pp. 183-191, April 1973.

17. See his comments in the series, Burlington's Investments Minimize the Hazard, *Charlotte Observer,* February 3-10, 1980. On ATMI's position, see [4, p. 125].

18. Interview conducted by Beardsley [3, p. 239]. Merchant confirms this comment. Merchant interview.

19. Both Imbus (lecture) and Donald Hayes (interview) imply that J. P. Stevens was well behind Burlington in its occupational health policies and practice. For a detailed discussion of the protest and boycott of J. P. Stevens, see *Rise Gonna Rise,* Anchor Press/Doubleday, New York, 1979, especially Part Five.

20. Both Beardsley and Botsch explain Burlington's actions as an attempt to enhance the company's image [3, pp. 239-240; 4, p. 132].

21. It must be emphasized, however, that cleaner mills were not simply a by-product of modernization, as Botsch, for example, suggests [4, p. 139]. During 1973-74, Burlington, in conjunction with outside contractors, developed specific dust reduction technology, the first "chute-fed carding system." Its concerns, then, were more than just modernization per se. See Michaels interview.

CHAPTER 11

Brown Lung and the Lessons for Occupational Health and Safety

By the early 1990s, state workers' compensation systems had paid out millions of dollars in claims for byssinosis. That amount represents only a small fraction of the cost to workers of this disease and, even more disturbing, relatively few workers actually received any benefits. Many were denied compensation, many did not file for compensation, many died before they could be awarded compensation. Had the disease been recognized earlier, more textile workers might have received help far sooner, more workers might have been spared the ravages of an agonizing disease. This is an American tragedy.

The disease was no secret to mill workers. They experienced it and named it, in their own way. But because of their lack of economic power and political organization, as well as their low social standing, they were unable to gain much attention from those with power, including and especially the scientific community. Only in unionized Massachusetts at the turn of the century were textile workers able to win the support of social reformers and public health workers—and then only on the terms of the mainstream and middle-class anti-tuberculosis movement. In the best of times, even in those rare historical moments when occupational health and safety take center stage, workers rely on health professionals to diagnose and define their illnesses in ways that can be acted upon.

Yet there are many players who have an interest in how a disease is defined; the naming of an occupational disease includes its industrial etiology and thus implies potential liability. Calling a disease "chronic bronchitis"—as was often claimed in the case of serious breathing problems among mill workers—implies no economics. Calling it "tuberculosis" shifts the costs to the public and away from employers. Calling it "byssinosis" has important financial consequences for employers. Potentially heavy financial burdens are usually involved in diseases from occupational sources, and these burdens, in turn, generate protective and

139

deflective social and political activity. Such was the case with byssinosis, where powerful interested parties and the relations among them shaped, constrained, and contained knowledge.

There were at least three points in the history of brown lung where the disease was uncovered, but it was not until its discovery in the late 1960s that it gained the critical mass that eventually produced public policy geared toward helping and protecting its victims. M. F. Trice and James Hammond discovered the problem in the field around 1940 while working on industrial hygiene problems in the Carolinas; the Harvard Cotton Dust Project acknowledged the existence of the disease by 1950 as part of its work on mill ventilation systems; Arend Bouhuys finally brought it to full scientific recognition in the late 1960s when he showed that a sizable number of American textile workers suffered from byssinosis. The Burlington studies forced the textile industry to admit, if begrudgingly, that the work processes in their mills were indeed responsible for byssinosis, but here we ask: Why did no ameliorating action follow the discoveries of 1940 and 1950? Why did Bouhuys have to mount such a momentous battle, decades after the earlier discoveries, merely to prove brown lung's presence in the United States?

The answer partly lies in the individual circumstances of each discovery.

Trice and Hammond located byssinosis in the field. Both made their findings from positions in the public health sector where they focused on industrial hygiene problems during wartime. Hammond's work was casual and informal and he never published anything about his findings; he collected information but did not disseminate it. Trice, though, took a more official posture regarding the disease, and drew the attention of his industrial hygiene office to the problems he saw. But he operated within a state framework, not at a national level.

He was alarmed enough that he wrote about his discovery of the textile industry disease, publishing a number of articles in trade publications but not voicing his concerns in first-rate, national or international, peer-reviewed scientific journals about health or medicine. Trice also tapped into the international literature to study Britain's experience with byssinosis, but his efforts to disseminate what he had learned were restricted to more local or industry-specific outlets, so much so that even Hammond, working in a neighboring state about the same time, apparently never saw any of Trice's work.

The publications Trice wrote for had little or no medical or public health audience. He undoubtedly reached industry owners through these publications, but they, of course, were an unreceptive and unwelcoming audience, hostile to the message he brought. In Trice's own words: "Textile men may be the last people in the world to admit that occupational diseases are a problem."

It appears that Trice knew how to gather scientific evidence, but did not know how to get his knowledge out to a significant audience with enough clout to act on it. His published work did not constitute a literature that was known to later scientists; it had not entered the mainstream of scientific literature.

As a result, a few years later, Drinker and the Harvard cotton dust researchers came separately to their own acknowledgment of the existence of byssinosis. It probably is not surprising that their conclusions had little impact. Drinker and his team's funding came from industry, and so they were working for and reporting to industry. In addition, they were basically engineers, not health specialists, and their work was oriented to the various aspects of exposure measurement and control and of ventilation, not to the health effects of cotton dust exposure.

Though Silverman and Viles came around to a somewhat ambiguous acknowledgment of byssinosis, it was a second-hand nod to the disease that was based on the review produced by B. H. Caminata, Silverman's experiences in England, and their own observations that some malady was present among the workers that bore an imprecise relationship to the dust levels in the mill rooms.

Drinker, Silverman, and Viles did not study the disease or the health effects from exposure—though perhaps they should have, given the published views of Drinker and Hatch on the nature of industrial surveys. Moreover, for whatever reasons, they seemed to identify more with the industrialists who funded them rather than the workers who might benefit from their work and knowledge of their work. In any event, when more interesting engineering challenges presented themselves, the team moved on.

Bouhuys had substantial advantages in his investigation of textile disease. When starting his U.S. research, he knew that byssinosis existed and he knew what it felt like. He had experienced the workers' "Monday morning feeling" firsthand in doing his aerosolized histamine-liberation test. He was a European who had ties to byssinosis researchers in Great Britain and elsewhere. Before coming to America he already had a strong personal commitment to byssinosis science and his work had already taken on a strong momentum. Finally, Bouhuys was a physician and scientist, with all the clout and prestige—as well as ethical standards—those titles imply.

When he landed in Atlanta to take up his byssinosis investigations, he was poised in the middle of the American textile industry at a time when local and state health officials had already independently developed their own interest in and concern about byssinosis, even though on their own they had made little progress. Bouhuys was not constrained in the same way that Georgia health officials were in their convoluted political relationships with local industry that hamstrung their investigative efforts. Moreover, Bouhuys began his work in the United States with funding from a prestigious federal health agency, precisely the kind of help that agency had denied to the Atlanta researchers only a short time earlier.

Professionally, while he maintained his international connections, Bouhuys was able to develop a national network of sources and contacts which eventually gave him access to such a pool of workers and a range of industrial circumstances that he was able to build evidence for his case. Bouhuys also sought publication in prestigious national science and medical journals and his work attracted prominent attention, as evidenced by his invitation from Dr. Irving Selikoff to speak before the New York Academy of Sciences.

Bouhuys was able to establish byssinosis as an American occupational disease. Research still had to establish the prevalence of the disease (Burlington), generate the dose/response relationships necessary for standard-setting, and determine the specific component or components of cotton dust that cause byssinosis, a task that has still yet to be accomplished. Over the past two decades or so, scientific inquiry has focused on the relationship between acute and chronic respiratory disease, the specific chronic diseases caused by cotton dust, and the role of smoking in causing respiratory disability in cotton mill workers. The debate over byssinosis, even at this late date, continues. But since the work of Bouhuys, no credible medical or scientific authority has contested the existence of byssinosis among cotton mill workers in this country.

Beyond the particular circumstances researchers found themselves in, however, they all operated within a basic truth, and this is perhaps the most important lesson to be learned from the history of the discovery of byssinosis in the United States. The key player in the industrial hygiene system is the employer, who controls the workplace, the worker, the technology, and the hazard. All other players—insurance carriers, government agencies, unions, scientists—gain access to the industrial situation through their relations with this central figure.

What accounts for employer power? Why were the interests of the workers not better represented? The first and obvious answers are the capitalist relations of production and the right of private property, which law and ideology in this country uphold and protect above all other rights. That said, the problem derives—to some extent—from the weakness of the workers' organizations, but the weakness of labor in the textile industry in the United States is not a unique situation. American trade unions more often than not take a defensive posture because the political and economic climate necessitates it, but also because—as necessity becomes convention—this is how mainstream American labor leadership has tended to see its role.

Unionists in the United States have seldom been able to mount serious attacks on owner and management prerogatives, and this is especially true, with some exceptions, in the area of workplace health and safety. As we discussed in Chapter 1, union, or government, attempts to regulate the workplace run counter to the interests of owners and mangers in maximizing profits and maintaining effective control of the workplace. Thus, as a general rule, owners and managers will vehemently resist such imprecations.

This is not to say that organized labor has never played a role in the fight for health and safety on the job. As we have seen, labor was instrumental in the suck shuttle ban; efforts by the Black Lung Association and later the United Mine Workers led directly to more stringent federal regulation of mines. Labor efforts contributed to the creation of OSHA, and in turn the creation of OSHA has allowed space in which organized labor might participate in the battles over workplace standards; such has been the case, for instance, in OSHA's efforts in recent years to implement an ergonomics standards, an effort that has, predictably, brought the full wrath of industry down upon OSHA, unions, and progressive health professionals.

Still, despite episodes to the contrary, labor in the United States long ago lost the battle for control of workplace technology and accommodated its goals and demands to this defeat.

For their part, health scientists seeking to investigate occupational illness and industrial hazards are handicapped by the need to access the work setting. Such investigators occupy a variety of positions in the industrial hygiene system: in government agencies, universities, insurance companies, even in industrial plants themselves. But no matter where they are located, they must deal with this fundamental need for access. They may face fundamental conflicts between this need and their professional responsibilities and ethics. In certain settings, they may find themselves constrained in their actions not only by the owners or managers of the workplace, the gatekeepers of access, but also by their own employers and superiors. Finally, they may be constrained by their own needs and desires for career advancement and material security. No other area of health science faces such a large number of obstacles to scientific discovery.

Private control of the workplace engenders a complex web of political and economic relations among the players in occupational health. Within this web are conditioned the nature and interpretations of a study, the questions asked, the ability to publish results, even the attention paid to the findings. Thus, an elaborate social, scientific, and economic structure is built on the misery of the exposed and endangered workers who are the subjects of these studies. And even though it is their physical and economic well-being that is at stake, the parameters of such studies are set within relations far beyond the workers' reach.

Industrial migration from the North, the subsequent decline of textile unionism, employer domination of Southern mill communities, and doctors' ignorance of occupational medicine practices are factors that also help explain the long delay in the recognition of byssinosis. But the history of brown lung is no mere marginal, sad tale of a particularly oppressed group of workers, in a peculiarly domineering and paranoid industry, in a "backward" region of the United States. This is perhaps too easy and comforting an interpretation. This history tells us something more fundamental, and troubling, about the nature of the relationship between workplace health hazards and health science, between economic power and public health.

In the story of brown lung, industry was able simply to ignore the warnings of Trice. Through his own words, Hammond acknowledged that the power of the mill owners limited what he could do: "Conditions were set for you, and the terms on which the game had to be played."

The Harvard team led by Drinker produced only a gentle prod to industry that had no discernible effect. As far as sharing their research with workers or their representatives was concerned, team member Silverman made very clear his reservations about trade union involvement in technological choices for the mills when writing to his funding source, Saco-Lowell.

Insurers had a special role in the history of brown lung. Next to industry itself, they were the substantial institution with an intimate connection to industry that gave them access to industrial facilities and workers. Liberty Mutual had an announced interest in occupational safety and health—improvement in these areas was, after all, one of the rationales for the creation of the state workers' compensation system in the first place. Health professionals at Liberty Mutual knew about byssinosis and knew that it was endemic in Southern cotton mills. They did not publish what they knew but the evidence shows that they discussed it with their client textile companies, then looked the other way and allowed their clients to do the same; they were "running from it, really." In the 1950s, officials at Liberty Mutual refused to cooperate with state investigators when asked to identify companies that might have a problem with byssinosis. For Liberty Mutual to have acted otherwise, industry would have had to release it from its business obligation of confidentiality. But the economic stakes were too high, the bonds of business relations to tight, for that to happen. Business relations overrode the well-being of endangered workers, and brown lung remained a secret.

The private control of the work environment by mill owners repeatedly thwarted the efforts of government investigators. Ted Forbes and the Georgia Textile Manufacturers Association were able to keep state health officials such as Petrie, Dickson, and Venable at bay simply by refusing them entry to the mills and making sure that no wavering GTMA member caved in and allowed such access. This lack of cooperation among the mill owners of Georgia helped doom Dickson's application for funding from the National Institutes of Health.

If the State of Georgia had been able to compel companies to cooperate with health officials—a power it most certainly did not have—the long road to the discovery of byssinosis would have been shorter, medical recognition would have come earlier. As it was, in a clever bit of legerdemain, the GTMA was able to steadfastly claim that no such disease as byssinosis existed in this country, even though no systematic epidemiological study of the health effects of cotton dust exposure had yet been conducted. But they were able to make this claim precisely because no systematic epidemiological study of the health effects of cotton dust exposure had been allowed to be conducted, and on the basis of this claim GTMA was able to block Bouhuys' access to cotton mills in Georgia.

The only way occupational health professionals could enter privately owned workplaces to investigate serious public health problems was by giving up control of their work, allowing industry officials to review their findings, allowing industry officials to have veto power over publication of their findings. On the private side, such was the case with the Harvard Cotton Dust Project, though industry control does not seem to have always been strictly enforced in this case. On the public side, Schrag was continually frustrated by Fieldcrest's unwillingness to allow publication of his study. When he threatened to publish the study anyway, he was warned by a highly placed and highly respected government epidemiologist, Alexander Langmuir, that he was on a "suicidal course." Langmuir, in turn, seems to have been motivated by a professional ethos which stressed cooperation with the textile industry and going through "official channels" and also by a desire not to offend the North Carolina State Health Department.

And so it went. At each stage of the long history of brown lung the private control of the workplace, the need among researchers for access, and the complex web of relations these factors generated played a central role.

Up to the era of the discovery of byssinosis in the United States, scientific investigators and health professionals pursued their careers by fulfilling their obligations to their employers or funders and working to meet professional or scientific standards of practice. A responsible professional life required that they balance ethical considerations, obligations to clients, ideas about agency mission. At times they may have been unaware of the conflicts inherent in their position, at times they were and had to face obvious and painful choices.

Plainly, the history of brown lung shows that in too many cases the health professionals' obligations to employers and bureaucracy and to clients took precedence over their concerns for worker health and safety. Workers, without either political or economic power, were at the mercy of their employers and were not defended by the health professionals upon whom they should have been able to depend.

But the brown lung story is also one of stressed investigators, certain a hazard existed, forced into a position of coaxing and cajoling their way into the workplace, usually with little or no success. Whether their efforts led to results or not, they all showed a dogged determination to find out why mill workers were getting sick and what might be done to prevent this. To our minds, Trice and Hammond, investigators in the Department of Health of Georgia in the 1950s and early 1960s, investigators in the North Carolina Department of Health in the 1960s, Bouhuys, Schrag, Lumsden, and Merchant are heroes in this story.

No matter how occupational health professionals responded to the contra-dictory conditions they found themselves within, all faced tough questions. In light of the history we have presented in this book, these are neither abstract nor academic questions, but vital considerations that remain relevant and important today.

Does a health scientist meet professional and ethical obligations if he or she publishes findings in obscure scientific journals? Are ethical standards met when a government industrial hygienist warns industry officials about an occu-pational hazard but fails to warn workers? Should medical professionals who work for insurers honor company requests for confidentiality about hazards? If they do, how might crucial information become known; who will warn the worker-victims? Should health investigators routinely inform workers and their representatives—unions—about their findings? Should they leak information to workers, unions, the media? How does the health scientist balance the rival claims of science, clients, employers, financial supporters, and workers? Finally, what might make all these choices easier? This question we return to below.

A final lesson of the brown lung story is that science, by itself, was able to effect little change in the conditions that kept the disease a more or less "open secret." Not until a foreign investigator whose training and reputation were rooted in Europe entered the American scene and, simultaneously, the political and economic context of that scene changed quite drastically, did serious, meaningful action on byssinosis occur. Changes in workplace conditions in the mills only took place in the context of the development of political activism and social reform movements of the late 1960s, when a close link was forged between public health scientists and the burgeoning social and labor movements of the time, much as had happened in the banning of the suck shuttle. It was only in this context that the achievements and discoveries of science made a difference and brown lung appeared on the national agenda for change. The discovery of byssinosis in the United States was a scientific outcome of the political turbulence of the 1960s.

The civil rights struggle, labor's resurgence and the fight for OSHA, the rise of consumer-worker advocacy, the development of the environmental movement—all altered the context in which the industrial hygiene system generated knowledge. A crack in employer domination—first started by Bouhuys and to a lesser degree Schrag, widened by the efforts of Lumsden and Merchant, and fully opened by Burlington's capitulation to the new political, social, and economic forces swirling around it—permitted a "new" occupational disease to emerge.

Occupational health science, then, operates at all times within a highly politicized context. The nature of this context will have much to do with what this science will ask or be allowed to ask, and how its discoveries will be used, or not used. We have stressed time and again in this work the importance of the emergence of particular historical forces or actors for significant change to occur in the realm of occupational health, and have consciously bookended our study with stories of two such episodes, precisely to illuminate the above points concerning occupational health science.

We do not wish to imply, however—and in fact emphatically reject the notion—that significant social change is and can only be the result of serendipitous historical convergences that we simply sit around and wait for. Rather, we highlight these episodes to demonstrate what it takes for significant social change to occur in the United States, and in order to learn valuable lessons that might be applied to future struggles.

At the most basic level, the relations of production within capitalism and the ceaseless search for profits by owners and mangers within these relations will always generate crises and resistance to these crises. But the conditions that allow such resistance to reach a critical mass, engender societal wide consciousness, and actually succeed in reigning in the power of capital is another matter.

Clearly, in the area of occupational health American labor alone cannot achieve such outcomes. A weakened labor movement does not have the power to command the attention of scientists, nor can it weigh heavily in the science politics of government agencies. For their part, occupational health professionals, given the constraints of the political milieu in which they all too often must operate, cannot by themselves be powerful agents for change.

For advocates of workers' health there is an obvious answer to these dual dilemmas: the public health community should move to a high place on its legislative and public policy agenda the development of public support for workers' rights to organize and maintain trade unions of their own choosing. A vibrant, democratic labor movement is essential to occupational health and safety promotion. A strong labor movement can also offer a supportive setting when, as we have noted above is often the case, occupational health professionals must decide whose interests they must ultimately serve; balancing the rival claims of science, clients, employers, financial supporters, and workers might become an easier task.

Yet the labor movement needs not only the political support of public health professional organizations (and they of the labor movement), but also its own scientists, people who fully understand the situation of the workers, who are committed to advancing worker health, and who are not dependent on outside funding. Labor must have its own physicians and epidemiologists, industrial hygienists and safety engineers, institutes and educational programs. The labor movement should use its political influence to create sympathetic enclaves in public institutions of higher education and research, but that will not substitute for its own personnel and institutions.

Labor must help build coalitions, work with environmental groups, community organizers, grassroots activists; all of whom, as during the late 1960s, might find common ground in the struggle for a safer work environment. Labor must expand its membership, recruiting members from more diverse populations and occupations. It must experiment with new organizing strategies, working, for example, within communities or across industries.

Unions are in fact organizing once again. But will such organizing continue along the old lines of bureaucratic, "card signing" strategies, or will grassroots, militant, highly democratic and participatory institutions be allowed to emerge? Within the latter strategy of broad-based social unionism, workplace health and safety will play an important organizing role and be a significant element in grassroots struggle for the empowerment of workers, and all people, and for real improvements in the quality of their lives.

By such measures, then, might a strong, sustained social force be created that would be highly conducive to gains in occupational health. Still, it must be remembered that within the relations of production as they now stand, the employer remains the key player in the industrial hygiene system. And while we cannot rule out that employers will take progressive measures in the area of workplace health simply because it is the right thing to do, we cannot assume that to be the case. Certainly since the creation of OSHA, employers have in general had somewhat less autonomy in creating workplace conditions, but OSHA is a small agency with a minuscule budget and few inspectors, and its powers and prerogatives are under constant political challenge. As we write this, for instance, the House of Representatives has voted to prohibit OSHA from issuing final ergonomic rules, rules that might prevent hundreds of thousands of workplace injuries.

As the history of brown lung and, to a somewhat lesser degree, that of the suck shuttle ban make clear, employers are most likely to adopt strong workplace health measures when it is in their economic interests to do so, when it makes good business sense. And, if one member of a particular industry breaks ranks and adopts such measures, there is strong pressure for other members to follow suit.

But such breaking of ranks—and we cannot stress this enough—is dependent upon the degree of public pressure there is to do so. It is thus no accident that it was in the late 1960s—not in the 1940s or the 1950s—that Burlington Industries decided to open up their mills to full epidemiological investigations and publicly admitted that cotton dust caused byssinosis.

It is not the case that improvement in workplace health and safety necessarily comes about as either a direct result or a by-product of technological innovation and progress (just as it is not the case that the recognition of an industrial disease comes about due to the slow but steady dispassionate accretion of scientific knowledge). To our mind, this is an odd sort of technological determinism that ignores the political and economic context of technological change.

To be sure, such technological improvement is essential to a safer and healthier work environment. But technological innovation in the hands of private owners first and foremost must improve productivity and profits—such innovation is not by nature geared toward nor concerned with worker health and safety. Although such technological change may improve the conditions of the workplace, they can also cause those conditions to deteriorate. Air conditioning improved conditions in the mills to a degree, the mechanization of cotton picking produced dirtier cotton for mill workers to handle. It is also of note that technological improvement in industry in the early decades of this century led to a virtual epidemic of workplace injury and disease.

In our view, then, the history of brown lung shows that a firm will most likely break ranks with others in its industry, admit to a health problem in the workplace, act to ameliorate that problem when it faces a coalition of progressive social actors that forces it to see such moves as being in their self-interest. Which firm will break ranks depends on a variety of factors, most prominently a dominant position in the industry and a degree of technological sophistication that will make it relatively cheaper to address health and safety issues.

The strategies and suggestions we have discussed above—mutual support between unions and the public health community, the recruitment by unions of their own health care professionals, cooperation among unions and community and grassroots activist organizations, vigorous and innovative union organizing— are all today realities in this society. Some have had true success, others are at the fledgling stage; and if these various social forces have not yet once again coalesced into a powerful progressive force, the potential is there. How well we struggle for democracy and economic justice will in the end determine how healthy, how safe, how happy our lives will be both in the workplace and in the community.

The history of brown lung bares the fact that economic motives and economic power can and do have a profound impact on the development of knowledge within occupational health science and that bureaucratic constraints and motives can keep serious problems quite secret. The history of brown lung also shows that the keeping of such secrets can cause diminished lives and agonizing deaths among generations of working people.

The recognition of brown lung and the passage of the Occupational Safety and Health Act did not stem the epidemic of occupational disease in this country. A host of other hazards, some associated with new technologies and some the same old problems of well-worn technologies, continue to take their toll in morbidity and mortality.

If brown lung remained a dark secret for generations, it was—and is—not the only one.

Index